The Great Deception

The Great Deception

And What Jesus Really Said and Did

Gerd Lüdemann

SCM PRESS LTD

Translated by John Bowden from the German
Der grosse Betrug. Und was Jesus wirklich sagte und tat, published 1998 by zu Klampen Verlag, Lüneberg, with additional material by the author.

0 334 02747 0

First published 1998 by
SCM Press Ltd
9–17 St Albans Place London N1 0NX

Typeset by Regent Typesetting, London
Printed in Great Britain by
Biddles Ltd, Guildford and King's Lynn

This book is dedicated to
A.-J. Levine

Contents

Preface

From the beginnings of the church to the present day countless Christians have appealed to Jesus. In so doing they have simply been reading their own wishes into him. This devastating verdict does not first apply to the interpreters of Jesus in most recent times, but already to the authors of the biblical writings. So if already in the New Testament the majority of the sayings and actions of Jesus were put into his mouth or attributed to him subsequently, now it is time to identify the most important of those indisputably inauthentic sayings and actions of Jesus in a form which can be generally understood and at the same time make a selection from the few surviving authentic sayings and actions of Jesus on which there is a consensus. That is the purpose of the present book. At the same time it serves as a popular summary and announcement of a major work on Jesus which contains analyses of all the sayings and actions of Jesus that have been handed down and gives a well-founded verdict on the authenticity or inauthenticity of every single verse of the four New Testament Gospels and the newly-discovered ancient Gospel of Thomas. This book will appear next year under the title *Jesus after Two Thousand Years. What He Really Said and Did.*

At the same time the present book gives an account of why I myself must from now on regard as illegitimate any return to the preaching of Jesus as a foundation for Christian faith. I honestly regret the utterly inadequate attempts that I have made in this direction in the past, but I unreservedly stand by the historical analyses or reconstructions that I have presented in my previous books. I therefore ask now that they should be read exclusively in the spirit of the statement that is made at the end of the first chapter of this book. But if this is to be the basis, the only term that can be applied to the biblical phenomenon discussed here, namely to put one's own beliefs into the mouth of Jesus – in a pious but unscrupulous way – is 'deception'. And that is a term which the Jewish contemporaries of Jesus and the apostles already used (cf. Matt. 27.64).

Without the help of Frank Schleritt this work could never have been finished. I am grateful to Silke Röthke, my secretary of many years, for producing the manuscript, and to Dr Jürgen Wehnert for making numerous comments on the German original. I thank my friend Eugene TeSelle for a final look at the manuscript and my friend Dr John Bowden for the great care with which he has translated the book. Since I have added material to it and corrected some mistakes, this book is a new edition of the German original.

My former Vanderbilt colleague A.-J. Levine has allowed me to dedicate this book to her. Over the years she has encouraged me to continue relentlessly to pursue historical questions and to formulate my own viewpoint. Here is the result.

Göttingen, 27 April 1998
Gerd Lüdemann

I

A Letter to Jesus

Dear Lord Jesus,

That is how I have addressed you since my childhood, and that is what I have said for years as a grace before meals ('Come, Lord Jesus, be our guest . . .'). I have kept saying another prayer ('Lord Jesus, Son of the living God, have mercy on me') every evening as a magical formula, although I didn't really know why I was doing so. But it is precisely for that reason that calling you 'Lord Jesus' has left such a deep impression on me. I have also still gone on praying to you like this as the Lord Jesus in later times out of habit, thoughtlessness and anxiety, although I had long known that you were quite different from what my parents, my teachers and my pastor gave me to understand. You've become quite strange to me as a person whom I can address. For you didn't say or do most of the things which the Bible tells us that you said or did. Moreover you aren't at all the one depicted by the Bible and the church tradition. You weren't without sin and you aren't God's Son. You didn't at all want to die for the sins of the world. And what was particularly painful for me, you didn't institute the eucharist which for years I celebrated every Sunday in memory of you. The bread which

I ate wasn't your body, and the wine which I drank wasn't your blood. It was only my longing which hoped for all this. It relied completely on the servants of your church. But instead of taking seriously my doubt as to whether, almost like a cannibal, I was really to eat your flesh and really to drink your blood – as a Jew *you yourself* were strictly forbidden to consume blood – they referred me to Martin Luther's declaration: the holy eucharist 'is the true body and blood of our Lord Jesus Christ, appointed for us Christians by Christ himself to eat and drink under the bread and wine'.

But they have been wrong in laying claim to you. For you were quite different. You drove out demons like a magician and saw in this the advent of the kingdom of God. You had intimate contact with the devil and finally saw him falling like lightning from heaven. You expected the collapse of the whole world in the near future, and this was finally to give place to the new kingdom of God. For a while you and your followers led an insecure itinerant life in the service of the kingdom of God and taught a grandiose code of behaviour which interprets the Law of Moses in the light of love and thus embodies the best traditions of Israel. This includes your ethical maxims, which also embrace the enemy in love, and your daring parables, which show heroes, truly human heroes, engaged in crookery.

But none of this is any use: you too died, in the prime of life. You too drank the cup of death, indeed had to drink it – in a way that you didn't foresee. Despite profound experiences with your God, whom you called a father to be trusted and from whom you expected almost everything, your hopes for the future also died. They clashed with brutal reality. At the latest on the cross you had to learn what it means to become a godforsaken victim. And had not your followers, who were understandably inspired by you, proclaimed belief in your resurrection, all your words and deeds would have been blown away like leaves by the wind. Moreover had they not proclaimed your imminent return for judgment and eternal salvation, the whole structure of Christian thought would soon have fallen in on itself.

But you did not return, because your resurrection did not even take place, but was only a pious wish. That is certain, because your body rotted in the tomb – that is, if it was put in a tomb at all and was not devoured by vultures and jackals. Certainly your followers used belief in the resurrection and your return to ward off despair after the shock of Good Friday, but today? Christians still – or today again – cling to your resurrection, though many have long since left behind the original meaning of resurrection. It is conceded that your body was not revived, and they prefer to talk of your being with God. At the same time bishops, educated church functionaries and Christian intellectuals, who sometimes even include professors of theology, think it important to maintain the confession of the resurrection, regardless of what may be understood by it. But this intellectual obfuscation is bound to come to grief and needs to be shown up ruthlessly. No authentic religion can be built on projections, wishes and visions, not even if it appears in such a powerful form as that of the Christian church, which has even exalted you to be the Lord of the worlds and coming judge. But you are not the Lord of the worlds, as your followers declared you to be on the basis of your resurrection, nor did you want to be. You proclaimed the future kingdom of God, but what came was the church. You deceived yourself, and your message has been falsified by your supporters for their own advantage, contrary to the historical truth. Your teaching was a mistake, since the messianic kingdom did not materialize.

Please look at all the crimes which have been committed in your name from your death to the present day. They already begin in the New Testament, where your fellow countrymen are called sons of the devil, simply because they do not believe in you. What is infamous here is that these words of condemnation are put on your lips, as though *you* had spoken them. This anti-Judaism then continues throughout church history. It is certainly not a deviation from the original teachings of the church; no, it had to develop *because* you had been exalted to become ruler of the world. From then on, from heaven and on behalf of your omnipotent Father, you punished the unbelieving Jews for their unbelief, for their disobedience and for the misdeeds which they were said to have committed against you and your churches. Don't say that it was all a mistake and a falsification of your message! Rather, the Christian church *had to be* like this – as emerges from its two-thousand-year history; otherwise it would not have taken shape at all, and its mere existence would have been impossible and quite superfluous. Therefore we really cannot get down to the business of the day and from now on proclaim your true message as though the last 2000 years had not happened.

I feel great sympathy for your fellow countrymen, who have been able to rediscover you as their own brother in our time through the results of historical research, without adopting the church's teaching of your resurrection and your return. But at the same time I myself see no reason for now becoming a Jew. I personally am still too shocked at the zealous God Yahweh of the Old Testament, who is utterly intolerant and whom the Christians then made use of to drive the Jews out of God's vineyard. This Yahweh does not know any equality of all peoples, nor does he recognize any rights which everyone in the world enjoys in the same way. Therefore I am firmly convinced that our German Basic Law, with articles protecting human dignity, the rights to freedom, to equality under the law, to freedom of belief, conscience and opinion, protects the life of all men and women more than the Bible of the Jews (the Old Testament) and indeed the Bible of the Christians (the Old and New Testaments). Certainly church leaders and theologians today are emphasizing that the fundamental rights of our Basic Law which I have just mentioned are of biblical origin, but I ask myself why up to around the seventeenth century the church and theology did not develop any basic rights applying to *all* individuals, corresponding to the Basic Law, and why these, together with the notion of tolerance, had to be established by the Enlightenment, in a battle against the church which was sometimes bitter.

You certainly have my deep sympathy, Lord Jesus, but you can't understand me at all and we can't understand you, because the time in which you lived is so different from the time in which we live now. Perhaps you would have become pensive had you learned that heaven is not above you, that the earth is a globe and not the centre of the whole universe. And probably you would have been very suprised to learn that human beings and apes have common ancestors, indeed that all existing species of living beings are part of a development which began with primitive unicellular organisms. And you would certainly have panicked had you been aware that even 2000 years after you, your God had still not brought in an end of the ages.

And not only that: your God did not even create the world, as you had to assume as a pious Jew of your day. Rather, the universe came into being through an evolution which according to our present-day knowledge began with a Big Bang. The image of the creator God which you and your contemporaries had was shaped far too much from a human perspective, and that applies to a far greater degree to the servants of your church today. They should have known better, but nevertheless every Sunday they confess your God as Creator of heaven and earth. I would prefer to say that what holds our cosmos together and limits it is a great mystery. We shall not solve it, but it is worth investigating. I think that such an open view of things is incompatible with the assumption of a biblical creator God who created everything from nothing. And since you will perhaps ask in alarm how I deal with the reality which you and your followers called and continue to call your God, I want to tell you a dream which freed me from this super-father, not to say superstition.

I struggled with God. He was strong and wanted to drag me down into a chasm in which paralysis, guilt and anxiety were awaiting me. When I saw the chasm I recalled in a flash how much my life had once been governed by paralysis, guilt and anxiety. I said to myself, 'Never again', and I became strong as an ox. With the last of my strength I pushed God himself down into the mire and at last became free.

Even after this dream I made another attempt to separate the essence of your message from the time-conditioned features of your preaching. And I clung to your code of behaviour and the basis for it. I thought that elements of your preaching of non-violence, love of enemy and openness to the outcast remained valid. But these ethical maxims were also developed by others before you and are not unique. Moreover they presuppose the expectation of the imminent rule of your God, and that has proved an error. But above all, I now know that in my attempts to attach myself to you and understand you as the basis of my life, I was still secretly living from Easter, from your Easter image, which is based on the church's dogma. However, that has long since collapsed, and with it also your own authority for me.

In general I doubt whether the investigation of history, including your preaching, leads to the formation of a moral code which can be binding in the present day. The historical method which I have practised hardly provides a universal ethical meaning or guidelines for action. My previous belief in that evidently rested on projections or on a presupposition behind which I could not investigate. I cannot go on believing in the normative power of history or of historical facts without presenting my own subjective notions in the guise of scholarship. Moreover the code of behaviour which you lived out is conditioned by your situation and cannot be transferred to the present time. That means that we must ourselves form rules of behaviour with a rational basis which can depend neither on you nor on your heavenly Father nor on any other deity.

Professors of theology and bishops want at almost any price to avoid these conclusions, which follow from the collapse of the idea of a creation from nothing, from the hoax of your 'resurrection' and the impossibility of ethics on the basis of your preaching. They even think that they're doing you a favour here. That's how I too acted and thought for many years. But I was doing it for myself, in order to be able to keep my faith, to conquer my own anxiety and to continue to hold my position of power in the church sphere. However, my attempts to define your 'resurrection' as a experience of forgiveness, as an experience of eternity and an experience of life had to fail, because these experiences can also be had apart from your person and your 'resurrection', and do not depend on what you called God. So I prefer from now on to develop a purely human view of religion without having to legitimate myself by a higher authority which theologians call God. Through many discussions with colleagues about your 'resurrection' and its correct interpretation I became painfully aware that these colleagues wanted to remain theologians at any price and secretly kept referring to another reality, without directly addressing it in the discussion of texts, stories or experiences. I can no longer accede to this secret presupposition.

So, Lord Jesus, an end to all that. I can no longer bear the totally confused situation of theology, the church and the Bible. Remain where you are, in the Galilee of the first century. Then you will again become far more credible as a charismatic exorcist and distinguished teacher, and we can again enter into a normal relationship with you, as we have done with other normative figures of antiquity, like Buddha, Confucius and Socrates. Your exaltation above all human possibilities was too much and derives from boundless fantasies of immortality and longings which must now be brought down to earth.

But if you really should return on the clouds of heaven, I already look forward to getting to know you at last. And I am convinced, even if I no longer pray to you and no longer believe in you, that I will have your sympathy and that you will not annihilate me for my unbelief, as according to Bible and creed you really should. But until then, as far as religion is concerned, there must be a final end to things between us – for the reasons which I have mentioned to you.

I shall continue to investigate your preaching and the Christian interpretations attached to it – with the aim of enlightening contemporaries of the present day in understandable language about the real origin of our Western culture. For the Enlightenment, which is grounded in reason, with all its criticism of claims to revelation and privileged knowledge of every kind, remains a firm ingredient of the modern world. Only enlightenment makes possible a constructive dialogue between the members of the different nationalities and cultures, and it alone would be in a position in the coming millennium to make peace between people of the most different ideologies and religions.

II

How the Authenticity and Inauthenticity of Sayings and Actions of Jesus are to be Decided: Examples and Criteria

This book is written in the conviction that Christians must adopt a credible relationship to Jesus, and also that all other men and women in the cultural area shaped by the Christian West should check out historically the roots of Christianity in the person of Jesus of Nazareth. This question is vitally important for both groups in coping with their own history and shaping the future.

Now it is generally recognized that beyond doubt many words and actions were only attributed to Jesus in the early church after his death. Here first of all are just two examples:

(*a*) The 'I am' discourses in the Gospel of John which make Jesus say of himself in the first person that he is the resurrection, that he is the light of the world, the vine and so on, certainly do not go back to Jesus but were only attributed to him afterwards, to express the faith of a later generation of Christians.

(*b*) The same holds for most of the miracle stories.

Examples and Criteria

Nowadays hardly anyone seriously assumes that Jesus in fact walked on the sea, stilled a storm, multiplied loaves, turned water into wine and raised the dead. Rather, these narratives were credited to Jesus only after his death or his supposed resurrection in order to heighten his significance.

These better insights, which were first worked out by historical criticism, do not alter the fact that within the framework of the formation of the biblical canon the early Christians regarded all this as authentic and accordingly from then on also regarded inauthentic sayings and actions of Jesus as part of the core of holy scripture. Therefore rigorous clarity must be achieved about all the traditions of Jesus in early Christianity which claim to be authentic. It is necessary to clarify what Jesus really said and did, what really happened at the time and what was obviously added later. To this end, in the following chapters a selection of obviously inauthentic sayings and actions of Jesus and of sayings and actions which in all probability are authentic are presented in translation and commented on.

This procedure is grounded in the intellectual history of our Western culture, which can no longer be thought of apart from the discovery of the historicity of every age including our own. Here, in the framework of developing the awareness of truth characteristic of modern times, the question of what was real and what was not, but is only claimed to be real, has irrevocably become an element in our own lives which we take for granted.

Now occasionally it is argued that such an enterprise *(a)* overestimates our own possibilities of distinguishing between authentic and inauthentic; (*b*) comes to grief on the fact that scholarly verdicts about what is authentic and what is inauthentic differ widely; and (*c*) does not sufficiently take into account the fact that the spirit of Jesus can be contained in inauthentic Jesus traditions. Moreover, (*d*) the question of authenticity and inauthenticity are said to be irrelevant to faith, since one and the same Lord is speaking in the Jesus of history and the Christ of faith.

On (*a*): I do not understand this objection, especially as it cannot be denied that the Bible certainly contains inauthentic sayings of Jesus. But if that is the case, the attempt can, indeed must, be ventured to identify authentic sayings and actions of Jesus.

On (b): That there are different reconstructions of the words and actions of the historical Jesus is no argument against such an undertaking; multiplicity of opinions does not relieve us of the obligation to approach historical reality with the aim of achieving the utmost possible objectivity.

On (c): This cannot be disputed. But if we are to discover the spirit of Jesus, first of all it must be made quite clear where recognizably authentic traditions about Jesus are contained.

On (d): Any historical work can be contested with this theological argument, which has fundamentalist features. In fact it represents an attempt to overturn the historical consciousness of modernity, which still holds. This consciousness is vital, and, since the great confessions and religions have failed, is the one thing that is capable of leading to peace between human beings and their ideologies or religions. Historical consciousness is in any case a firm ingredient of our present-day world. Without this achievement of human culture no rational dialogue would be possible in politics, in business or in the private sphere. Why should it be that as soon as we enter the sphere of religions we should leave it behind? The result is well known: schizophrenia or a separation of science and religion.

Here are the *presuppositions* of my work:

The analyses of the way in which the three oldest New Testament Gospels are related is based on a modified two-source theory. That states that the Gospel of Mark is the earliest extant Gospel and comes from around the year 70. About twenty-five years later Matthew and Luke make independent use of both the Gospel of Mark and a discourse source (= Q) which might be as old as Mark. In addition, each has used his own special traditions.

The Gospel of John in its present form comes from the beginning of the second century and presupposes not only the Gospel of Mark but also the Gospel of Luke. At the same time it has incorporated special traditions.

The Gospel of Thomas, one of the discoveries made in Nag Hammadi in Upper Egypt in December 1945, which is to be dated to the same period as the Gospel of John, is certainly one of the written sources to be investigated here since, as is becoming increasingly clear, in part it reflects a tradition independent of the New Testament.

The present book gets by without explicit discussion of secondary literature. The basis for the exegetical decisions presupposed here will be given in the larger book mentioned in the Preface, which contains a translation and analysis of all the Jesus texts from the first two centuries.

Before the analysis of the traditions I want to mention some *criteria* for judgments on (*a*) the inauthenticity and (*b*) the authenticity of sayings and actions of Jesus.

(a) Criteria of inauthenticity

First, those sayings and actions are clearly inauthentic in which the exalted Lord speaks and acts or is presupposed as the one who speaks and acts. For Jesus himself no longer spoke and acted after his death. But as we cannot exclude the possibility that words or actions of the historical Jesus have been attributed to the 'Risen Christ' – for the early Christians the historical Jesus and the Christ of faith were identical – each time we must check whether particular sayings of the exalted Christ are not perhaps based on a saying of the earthly Jesus.

Secondly, those acts are unhistorical which presuppose that natural laws are broken. Here the fact that people in the time of Jesus did not know these laws or did not think in scientific categories is irrelevant.

Thirdly, a suspicion of inauthenticity attaches to all the sayings of Jesus if they give answers to community situations in a later time.

Fourthly, those sayings and actions are inauthentic which presuppose a Gentile (and not a Jewish) audience. For it is certain that Jesus was active exclusively in the Jewish sphere.

(b) Criteria of authenticity

First, many sayings and actions of Jesus might prove to be authentic by virtue of the criteria of offensiveness. For example, among Jesus' actions, his decision to be baptized by John belongs here. From very earliest times the baptism of Jesus was offensive to Christians, and from the beginning it was changed in various ways, passed over completely in silence or rejected by 'Jesus' himself (see below, pp.101f.).

Examples of offensive sayings of Jesus are the immoral heroes who appear strikingly often in his parables: the man who finds a treasure in a field and buys the field without reporting his discovery (Matt. 13.44), or the unjust steward who – when asked by his master to present the accounts – deceives him in order to find refuge among his master's debtors (Luke 16.1b–7). Finally, Jesus himself often acts as an immoral hero and has social dealings with prostitutes and toll collectors. This too is changed or 'interpreted' in the later tradition.

Secondly, the criterion of difference is a plausible way of discovering authentic Jesus material. Its use involves asking whether 'sayings of Jesus' can be derived from the post-Easter communities. If the answer to this is no, where there is a difference between the communities and Jesus, Jesus may be thought to have spoken the saying in question.

Thirdly, the criterion of growth offers a good opportunity of identifying authentic Jesus material. The final form of a text may be compared with an onion which can be peeled one skin after another. The older a unit of text is, the more deeply it is covered by later tradition. There are examples of this in the radical ethics of the Sermon on the Mount (see below, pp.88–91).

Fourthly, the criterion of rarity may be mentioned: this relates to those actions and sayings of Jesus which have only a few parallels (if any) in the Jewish sphere. Candidates for this are Jesus' absolute prohibition of oaths (Matt. 5.34a) or his absolute prohibition against judging (Matt. 7.1).

Fifthly, the criterion of coherence can be used to elicit authentic sayings of Jesus. Each time this asks whether a particular saying or action can be fitted seamlessly into assured Jesus material.

I shall now show how the criteria of inauthenticity and authenticity just mentioned can be used fruitfully, by means of two examples: the parable of the sower and the parable of the weeds among the wheat, along with their interpretations.

Mark 4.3–20
The parable of the sower and its interpretation

In Mark 4.3–8 Jesus tells the following parable:

> '3 A sower went out to sow.
> 4 And it happened that as he sowed, some seed fell
> along the path, and the birds came and devoured it.
> 5 Other seed fell on rocky ground, where it had not
> much soil, and immediately it sprang up, since it had no
> depth of soil. 6 And when the sun rose it was scorched,
> and since it had no root it withered away.
> 7 Other seed fell among thorns, and the thorns grew up
> and choked it, and it yielded no grain.
> 8 And other seed fell into good soil and brought forth

grain, growing up and increasing and yielding thirtyfold and sixtyfold and a hundredfold.'

The interpretation given shortly afterwards (Mark 4.14–20) goes like this:

'14 The sower sows the word.
15 And these are the ones along the path. Where the
word is sown and when they hear, Satan immediately
comes and takes away the word which has been sown in
them.
16 And these are the ones sown upon the rocky ground.
When they hear the word, they immediately receive it
with joy; 17 and they have no root in themselves, but
are unstable. Then, when tribulation or persecution
arises on account of the word, they take offence.
18 And others are the ones sown among thorns. They
are those who hear the word, 19 but the cares of the
world, and the seduction of riches, and the desire for
other things, enter into them and choke the word, and it
becomes unfruitful.
20 But those that were sown upon the good soil are the
ones who hear the word and accept it and bear fruit,
thirtyfold and sixtyfold and a hundredfold.'

There is no way in which this interpretation can go back to Jesus. This is why:

First, it is stamped by Christian terminology. For example, the absolute use of the term 'the word' is a designation for the gospel first used by the primitive church. In keeping with this, in the small section vv.14–20 we find a wealth of statements about the word which are alien to the rest of Jesus' preaching but common in a later period: the preacher spreads the word; the word is received – with joy; persecution arises because of the word; the word becomes offensive; the word grows; the word brings forth fruit.

A *second* reason why the interpretation in Mark 4.14–20 cannot go back to Jesus lies in the observation that words occur in this text which do not appear elsewhere in the three earliest Gospels but which are familiar to the rest of the New Testament literature: e.g. 'sow' in the transferred sense for 'proclaim'; 'root' in the transferred sense of inner steadfastness.

Thirdly, in addition to these linguistic points there is the weighy observation that the interpretation of the parable has been shifted one-sidedly in a psychological direction. In the interpretation the parable becomes an admonition to the newly converted to examine their hearts to see whether they have been truly converted.

The compelling conclusion to be drawn from this is that the interpretation of the parable of the sower in Mark 4.14–20 comes from the primitive church. The church saw this parable as an allegory and accordingly expounded it feature by feature. First of all the seed becomes the word which is being preached by the primitive church, then in a kind of table the four types of soil described are interpreted as four groups of people. Here two originally quite different thoughts have been behind the approach: on the one hand the comparison between the divine word and God's seed, and on the other the comparison of men and women with God's planting.

So here is a clear case where words have been put into the mouth of Jesus which he did not speak. Granted, the judgment that the interpretation of the parable certainly does not go back to Jesus does not in itself mean that the *parable itself* comes from Jesus. That would still have to be checked. Here it is important first of all simply to show that the interpretation of the parable is a text which Jesus certainly could not have spoken. But if that is the case, the question immediately arises: How many such cases are there? Indeed, how many of the sayings of Jesus contained in the New Testament arose in this way? And what percentage of them may be authentic? This question becomes even more urgent when we look at the wider context in which the parable of the sower and its interpretation stand.

Between the interpretation of the parable of the sower quoted above (Mark 4.14–20) and the parable itself there is the following explanation of why Jesus spoke in parables at all. Mark 4.10–12 reads:

> 10 And when he was alone, those who were about him
> with the Twelve asked him concerning the parables. 11
> And he said to them, 'To you has been given the secret
> of the kingdom of God. But for those outside everything
> happens in parables, 12 so that they may indeed see but
> not perceive, and may indeed hear but not understand,
> so that they do not turn again and are forgiven.'

Thus according to these verses Jesus speaks in parables with the express aim of preventing the hearers from being converted and forgiven (v.12). The contradiction between this statement and Jesus' real intention could not be greater. Whereas Jesus spoke in parables in order to be understood, the author of vv.10–12 makes him say quite the opposite: he has spoken in parables in order to be 'misunderstood'; in order to mislead 'those outside'.

This theory of hardening, which is put in the mouth of Jesus himself, goes back to the author of the Gospel of Mark or to his source, the viewpoint of which the author of the Gospel of Mark would have adopted. His statement in vv.11–12, the second part of which is a quotation of Isaiah 6.9–10, must be seen in the context in conjunction with those passages which go into Israel's unbelief. One might compare the decision of the Pharisees and Herodians to kill Jesus (Mark 3.6), the Pharisees' request for a sign (8.11), the question about Jesus' authority put by the high priests and scribes (11.27–33), and the fact that because of the killing of the son the vineyard will be taken away from Israel (by the destruction of Jerusalem in the year 70) (Mark 12.9); special emphasis is put on this last fact.

Positively, the saying in vv.11–12 corresponds to Peter's messianic confession (Mark 8.29) and the confession of the centurion under the cross (Mark 15.39). Both figures have recognized the mystery of the kingdom of God.

Matthew 13.24b–30, 37b–43
The parable of the weeds among the wheat and its interpretation

> '24 The kingdom of heaven is like a man who sowed good seed in his field. 25 But while the men were sleeping, his enemy came and sowed weeds among the wheat, and went away. 26 So when the plants came up and bore grain, then the weeds appeared also. 27 And the servants of the householder came and said to him, "Sir, did you not sow good seed in your field? How then has it weeds?" 28 He said to them, "An enemy has done this." The servants said to him, "Then do you want us to go and gather them?" 29 But he said, "No; lest in gathering the weeds you root up the wheat along with them. 30 Let both grow together until the harvest. And at harvest time I will tell the reapers, 'Gather the weeds first and bind them in bundles to be burned, but gather the wheat into my barn.'"'

To this parable, which appears only in his Gospel, the evangelist Matthew, following Mark, his model, adds the parables of the mustard seed (13.31–32) and the leaven (13.33). A little later, he relates that the disciples asked Jesus, 'Explain to us the parable of the weeds of the field' (v.36). Jesus replied to them:

> '37b He who sows the good seed is the Son of man; 38 the field is the *world*, and the good seed means *the sons of the kingdom*; the weeds are the sons of the evil one, 39 and the enemy who sowed them is *the devil*; the

harvest is the end of the age; and the reapers are angels. 40 Just as the weeds are gathered and burned with fire, so will it be at *the end of the age*. 41 The Son of man will send his angels, and they will gather out of his kingdom all those who give offence and do lawlessness, 42 and throw them into the furnace of fire; there will be weeping and gnashing of teeth. 43 Then the righteous will shine like the sun in the kingdom of their Father.'

It is impossible that this interpretation, too, came into being together with the parable; the parable and its interpretation go back to two *different* narrators. Here are the reasons:

First, nowhere does the interpretation touch on the key point of the parable: the admonition to patience.

Secondly, the interpretation is only selective, since neither the sleep of the men (v.25), nor the servants and their conversation with their master (vv.27–29), nor the barns (v.30) are interpreted.

Thirdly, Matt. 13.37b–43 displays a great accumulation of peculiarities of Matthaean language (the most important are printed in italics in the translation).

From these observations it follows that the interpretation goes back to another narrator than the 'Jesus' of the parable and may come from the evangelist Matthew himself, who has put his own view into the mouth of Jesus. Here Matthew is impressing on members of his community that they still face the judgment and that therefore they are summoned to right action in order to bring forth fruit.

These two striking examples may be enough to attest the urgency of the question of what Jesus really said. They are an impressive demonstration of how sayings of Jesus have already been interpreted in the Bible, though the interpreters preferred not to characterize their interpretation as their own but to put it directly into the mouth of Jesus himself. This is what has made it so difficult for later readers of the Bible to get to the historical truth, since any investigation of whether these are really sayings of Jesus has found itself confronted with the special status of the Bible as Holy Scripture. But it is no use: anyone who wants to get to Jesus – not Jesus as the early Christians depicted him but the man from Nazareth as he really was – must with a sharp mind first of all peel off all that has been put round sayings of Jesus, layer by layer, in the hope of thus getting back to the bedrock surrounding the authentic words of Jesus.

In using the term 'hope', however, I am indicating that as in the two examples cited, a parable given a later interpretation does not necessarily go back to Jesus himself. Rather, each time this possibility has to be examined further, on the basis of the reliable criteria mentioned above. At the same time the image of the bedrock makes it clear that in the most favourable instance we can only reach a high degree of approximation of the sayings of Jesus and not their absolutely final form. We come upon the bedrock, the immediate proximity, but not the sayings of Jesus himself. That must also be ruled out because Jesus spoke Aramaic and his sayings have been preserved only in Greek translation.

The same is true of the actions of Jesus: here, too, when it is said that this or that one is historically accurate, it can only be a matter of getting very near to what really happened at that time, since the narrative account of events always involves a reality, to a greater degree than the rendering of sayings into language.

So a decision about historicity is *not identical* with a decision about what Jesus really said or did. However, we may say that the decision about what is *'unhistorical'* is 'identical' with the decision about what he certainly did not say and what certainly did not happen. Still, these qualifications do not affect the value of the judgments made. Anyone expecting more here would get less.

Everything that goes beyond what has been said relates to the question of religious certainty, which is not the subject of this book. But my view is that the analyses made in this work are presuppositions for the religious question.

III

Inauthentic Sayings of Jesus

1. Jesus condemns Israel and its leaders

Matthew 23.13–28
Woes against scribes and Pharisees

First woe

'13 Woe to you, scribes and Pharisees, hypocrites!
because you shut the kingdom of heaven against men;
for you neither enter yourselves, nor allow those who
would enter to go in.

Second woe

15 Woe to you, scribes and Pharisees, hypocrites! for
you traverse sea and land to make a single proselyte, and
when he becomes a proselyte, you make him twice as
much a child of hell as yourselves.

Third woe

16 Woe to you, blind guides, who say, "If any one
swears by the temple, it is nothing; but if any one
swears by the gold of the temple, he is bound by his
oath." 17 You blind fools! For which is greater, the gold

or the temple that has made the gold sacred? 18 And you say, "If any one swears by the altar, it is nothing; but if any one swears by the gift that is on the altar, he is bound by his oath." 19 You blind men! For which is greater, the gift or the altar that makes the gift sacred? 20 So he who swears by the altar, swears by it and by everything on it. 21 And he who swears by the temple, swears by it and by him who dwells in it. 22 And he who swears by heaven, swears by the throne of God and by him who sits upon it.

Fourth woe

23 Woe to you, scribes and Pharisees, hypocrites! for you tithe mint and dill and cummin, and have neglected the most important matters in the Law, justice, and mercy and faith. These you ought to have done, without neglecting the others. 24 You blind guides, straining out a gnat and swallowing a camel!

Fifth woe

25 Woe to you, scribes and Pharisees, hypocrites! for you cleanse the outside of the cup and of the plate, but inside they are full of extortion and rapacity. 26 You blind Pharisee, first cleanse the inside of the cup, that the outside also may be clean.

Sixth woe

27 Woe to you, scribes and Pharisees, hypocrites! for you are like whitewashed tombs, which outwardly appear beautiful, but within they are full of dead men's bones and sheer garbage. 28 So you also outwardly

appear righteous to men, but within you are full of hypocrisy and iniquity.

Seventh woe

29 Woe to you, scribes and Pharisees, hypocrites! for
you build monumental tombs to the prophets and adorn
the graves of the righteous, 30 saying, "If we had lived
in the days of our fathers, we would not have been
guilty with them in shedding the blood of the prophets."
31 Thus you witness against yourselves that you are
sons of those who murdered the prophets. 32 Fill up,
then, the measure of your fathers. 33 You serpents, you
brood of vipers, how are you to escape the damnation
of hell?
34 Therefore, see, I send you prophets and wise men and
scribes, some of whom you will kill and crucify, and
some you will scourge in your synagogues and persecute
from town to town, 35 that upon you may come all the
righteous blood shed on earth, from the blood of
innocent Abel to the blood of Zechariah the son of
Barachiah, whom you murdered between temple and
altar. 36 Truly, I say to you, all this will come upon this
generation.
37 O Jerusalem, Jerusalem, you who kill the prophets
and stone those who are sent to you! How often
would I have gathered your children together as a hen
gathers her chicks under her wings, and you would not!
38 Behold, your house is forsaken and desolate.'

Explanation

Preliminary comment: verse 14 does not appear in the earliest manuscripts; it was formulated later on the basis of Mark 12.40 and is not an original part of the Gospel of Matthew.

Seven woes brand the scribes and Pharisees hypocrites (vv.13–33). Seven is a symbolic number indicating completeness. It often appears in the Gospel of Matthew (cf. simply 12.45) and is meant to increase the force of the charge even further. As Matthew found only six woes in the tradition, he composed the third woe himself and added it – as is evident from the somewhat different introduction.

The first woe is like a heading for the following six. In a general reckoning with the scribes and Pharisees Matthew declares that not only are they wrong on *individual* points but that they bar people's access to the kingdom of God *generally*. The picture of the opponents which follows has a negative colouring throughout and at the end of the seventh woe leads to the pronouncement of judgment: the measure is complete. The damnation of the scribes and Pharisees to hell is certain.

Whereas the preaching of judgment up to v.33 applied only to the scribes and Pharisees, in vv.34–36 the formal address to the scribes and Pharisees is dropped in order to hint at their successors after the destruction of Jerusalem. The Christian prophets, wise men and scribes (!) focus on Matthew's own day. They will suffer the fate of being killed, crucified and scourged (cf. Matt. 10.17; 22.6), at the hands of heirs of the Pharisees and scribes whom Jesus accused of hypocrisy. Verses 35f. show that Matthew is thinking of a judgment on all Israel. The lament over Jerusalem (vv.37f.) presupposes the punishment of the devastation of Jerusalem in the Jewish War, which took place only forty years after the death of Jesus. For the devastation of the city is not held out as a prospect here but is regarded as already having taken place: the city is *to continue to lie* in ruins.

The sharpness and polemic of Matthew's condemnations is made even more dubious by being attributed to Jesus himself and not being regarded as the view of Matthew or someone else. (Contrast Paul's remark in I Cor. 7.25 that he has no commandment from Jesus on a particular question; he then expressly indicates that what he says is his own view.)

Historical yield

Jesus cannot have spoken these woes, as they completely presuppose the situation of Matthew's community – or in the parts which he found already in existence (the six woes) the situation of a Christian community before him.

Matthew 21.33–46
The parable of the wicked tenants

'33 Hear another parable. There was a householder who planted a vineyard, and set a hedge around it, and dug a wine press in it, and built a tower, and let it out to tenants, and went abroad.
34 Now when the season of fruit drew near, he sent his
servants to the tenants, to get his fruit. 35 And the

tenants took his servants; they beat the first, killed the second, and stoned the third.
36 Again he sent other servants, more than the first time; and they did the same to them.
37 Lastly he sent his son to them and said to himself,
"They will respect my son." 38 But when the tenants
saw the son, they said to one another, "This is the heir;
come, let us kill him and have his inheritance." 39 And
they took him and cast him out of the vineyard, and killed him.
40 When therefore the owner of the vineyard comes, what will he do to those tenants?'
41 They said to him, 'He will prepare a wretched end for those wretches, and let out the vineyard to other *tenants who will give him the fruits in their seasons.*'
42 Jesus said to them, 'Have you never read in the Scriptures, "The very stone which the builders rejected has become the head of the corner. This was the Lord's doing, and it is marvellous in our eyes"? (Ps. 118.22,
23). 43 *Therefore I tell you, the kingdom of God will be*
taken away from you and given to a nation producing
the fruits of it. 44. And he who falls on this stone will be
broken to pieces; but when it falls on any one, it will crush him.'
45 And when the chief priests and the Pharisees heard his parables, they recognized that he was speaking about
them. 46 And they tried to seize him; but they feared the
people, because they held him to be a prophet.

Explanation

Matthew 21.33–46 transforms the text Mark 12.1–12 into a sketch of salvation history from the making of the covenant on Sinai (cf. v.33) through the destruction of Jerusalem (v.41: cf. Matt. 22.7) and the founding of the church of the Gentiles (v.43) to the last judgment (v.44). A particular emphasis in Matthew's interpretation becomes clear in two additions to the text of Mark which are printed in italics in the translation given above:

(a) In Matthew's version, Mark 12.9, 'The lord of the vineyard . . . will give the vineyard to others' becomes 'He will let out the vineyard to other tenants who will give him the fruits in their seasons' (Matt. 21.41).

(b) Matthew adds the clause 'Therefore I tell you, the kingdom of God will be taken away from you and given to a nation producing the fruits of it' (21.43) to the text of Mark. That means that God's kingdom will be taken away from Israel and given to a people which brings forth 'fruits of the kingdom of God'. The word 'people' denotes Gentiles and is also used at other points of the Gospel of Matthew where these are certainly meant (cf. Matt. 10.5, 'way of Gentiles'; 28.19, 'make disciples of all the Gentiles'). In other words, Matthew heightens all the anti-Jewish statements in Mark 12.1–12, the text which he uses, by explicitly emphasizing the handing over of the vineyard to the Gentiles and denying Israel any promise. From now on the church is regarded as the elect people and enters into the heritage of the disobedient Israel.

Historical yield

The parable certainly does not go back to Jesus, since first Matthew is working over a literary model (he was not an eye-witnesses), and secondly this text too can be explained completely from the situation of his community. The words are inauthentic.

Matthew 22.1–14
The parable of the wedding feast

1 And Jesus began and again spoke to them in parables, saying, '2 The kingdom of heaven may be compared to a king who gave a marriage feast for his son. 3 And he sent his servants to call those who were invited to the marriage feast; but they would not come. 4 Again he sent other servants, saying, "Tell those who are invited, Behold, I have made ready my dinner, my oxen and my fat calves are killed, and everything is ready; come to the marriage feast." 5 But they scorned this and went off, one to his field, another to his business. 6 And some seized his servants, treated them shamefully, and killed them.
7 *Then the king became angry, and he sent his troops and destroyed those murderers and burned their city*. 8 Then he said to his servants, "The wedding is ready, but *those invited were not worthy*. 9 So *go out on to the streets*, and invite to the marriage feast as many as you find." 10 And the servants *went on to the streets* and gathered all whom they found, both bad and good; and the tables were all filled.

11 But when the king came in to look at the guests, he
saw there a man who had no wedding garment; 12 and
he said to him, "Friend, how did you get in here without a wedding garment?" But the man was speechless.
13 Then the king said to his servants, "Bind him hand
and foot and cast him into the outer darkness; there men
will weep and gnash their teeth." 14 For many are
called, but few are chosen.'

Explanation

The parable of the wedding feast follows that of the wicked husbandmen (21.33–46), the purpose of which, described above, is worth recalling: the church replaces Israel in so far as it keeps Jesus' words. Israel is totally disqualified and completely robbed of its salvation by the destruction of Jerusalem.

A similar intention can be noted in the parable of the wedding feast. So that they can be recognized more quickly, the anti-Jewish sections and their positive counterparts, those passages focussed on the Gentiles, are printed in italics.

The parable of the wedding feast is an allegory of salvation history, but this time, in contrast to the parable of the wicked husbandmen, for the most part the period of Easter is in view. There is virtually no reference to the period up to the appearance of Jesus. An allegory occurs where a text is truly understood only when all its main terms are transferred to another sphere. The king, i.e. God, makes a feast for his son, Jesus Christ. The invitation to the meal, which he tries to deliver several times, is each time addressed to the Jews. Here the first group of servants (v.3) stands for the prophets. The second group (v.4) denotes the apostles or missionaries; the maltreatment and martyrdom which some of them suffer at the hands of the Jews who are invited is expressed in v.6. The sending on to the streets (vv.9f.) suggests the mission to the Gentiles and the entry into the marriage hall (v.10b) suggests baptism. The vivid statement in v.7 shows a heightening of the anti-Judaism: the murderous Jews will be killed and their city (= Jerusalem) will be burned. Matthew can depict this by looking back to the Jewish War in 70 CE.

Like the parable of the wicked tenants, vv.11–14 inculcate the role of good works and are a further indication that Matthew is concerned with behaviour. For v.9, which relates the wholesale invitation of guests, could have given the impression of ethical indifference.

Historical yield

The parable certainly does not go back to Jesus, since its content can be explained completely from the situation of Matthew's community. It is inauthentic.

John 8.37–45
Jesus calls the Jews sons of the devil

'37 You know that you are the seed of Abraham; yet you seek to kill me, because my word finds no place in you. 38 I speak of what I have seen from my Father, and you do what you have heard from your father.'
39 They answered and said to him, 'Abraham is our father.'
Jesus said to them, 'If you were Abraham's children, you

would do Abraham's works. 40 But now you seek to kill
me, a man who has told you the truth as I have heard it
from God. This is not what Abraham did. 41 You do
the works of your father.'

They said to him, 'We were not born of out of wedlock:
we have one Father, God.'

42 Jesus said to them, 'If God were your Father, you
would love me, for I proceeded and came forth from
God; I did not come not of my own accord, but he sent
me. 43 Why do you not understand what I say? It is
because you cannot bear to hear my word.

44 *You have the devil for your father*, and you want to
do your father's desires. He was a murderer from the
beginning, and does not stand in the truth, because the
truth is not in him. When he lies, he speaks according
to his own nature; for he is a liar and the father of lies.
45 But because I tell the truth, you do not believe me.'

Explanation

The argument between Jesus and his Jewish opponents runs through the Gospel of John like a scarlet thread. This controversy comes to a head where Jesus tells them that they have the devil for their father (John 8.44). From the beginning of the Gospel of John, the Jews aim to kill Jesus (cf. only 5.18). This aim is also continued in the passages which follow the present text (cf. 10.31–39; 11.45–53; 19.7).

In the present text the unbelieving Jews are explicitly called children of the devil or sons of the devil. The argument between the Christians behind the Gospel of John and the unbelieving Jews reaches a climax which can hardly be surpassed. Doubtless the sharpness of the polemic is to be attributed to the fact that the Christians in the association of Johannine communities have fallen out with unbelieving Jews. To that degree these are time-conditioned statements. However, they are hardly rhetorical, nor are they just playing with words. The author beyond doubt means what he writes and writes what he means. So the text is a regrettable provisional climax to the anti-Jewish attacks in early Christianity.

Historical yield

Jesus did not speak the words attributed to him in the present text. They are to be derived completely from the situation of the community from which the Gospel of John comes, and thus are inauthentic.

2. Jesus observes the Law completely and requires his disciples to observe it correctly

Luke 16.17
The eternal validity of the Law

> 'It is easier for heaven and earth to pass away, than for one dot of the law to become void.'

Explanation

This saying stands in isolation in the train of thought in the Gospel of Luke. Before it comes the saying about taking the kingdom of God by storm (v.16: 'The Law and the Prophets were until John; since then the good news of the kingdom of God is preached, and every one enters it violently') and it is followed by a saying of Jesus about adultery (v.18: 'Every one who divorces his wife and marries another commits adultery, and he who marries a woman divorced from her husband commits adultery').

Exegetes have laboured endlessly to devise a smooth flow of thought between these three logia of Jesus – with little success. These difficulties have one advantage. They show that the saying in Luke 16.17 is a saying of Jesus which has been handed down in isolation and was known in the communities before the composition of the Gospel of Luke. (For the possibility of its derivation from Q see the next section on Matt. 5.17–20, here v.18.)

The saying in Luke 16.17 states the absolute validity of the Law. It is so rigorous that not even all Jews could have agreed with it. But here it is regarded as a saying spoken by Jesus and it was manifestly put forward by some of his adherents.

Historical yield

The saying derives from a situation in the community in which a fight had flared up between liberal and conservative Christians. The liberal Christians were probably members of Hellenistic communities; the apostle Paul, who was accused by conservative Christians of apostasy from the Law, is also to placed in such a community. People spread the rumour that Paul taught all Jews in the Diaspora to stop circumcising their sons (Acts 21.21). The Christians making these accusations belonged to the community from Jerusalem which, under the leadership of James, a brother of Jesus, increasingly adopted a conservative attitude towards the Law. In these conservative circles, such a rigorous saying as Luke 16.17 might have been attributed to Jesus. In order to defend their own position in the fight against Hellenistic Christians, they attributed the saying to Jesus out of hand.

Jesus can never have uttered the saying, even if we think that he made different statements about the Law in different situations, or if it is claimed that he showed an ambivalent attitude to the Torah which accentuated the Law and relativized it at the same time. Beyond doubt Jesus' commandment to love one's enemy is an accentuation of the Old Testament law about loving one's neighbour. But that accentuation is of a *different* kind from that to be found in this logion, since it has completely different consequences. Moreover the exclusiveness of the saying is too clear for it ever to have been uttered by Jesus, no matter what the situation. It no longer allows any openness. (For Jesus' criticism of the Law and his attitude to it cf. pp.87ff. below.)

Matthew 5.17–20
The New Righteousness

'17 *Do not think that I have come to abolish the Law*
and the Prophets; I have come not to abolish them but to
fulfil them. 18 For truly, I say to you, till heaven and
earth pass away not a (single) iota, not a (single) dot,
will pass from the law *until all is accomplished.* 19 Whoever then relaxes one of the least of these commandments and teaches men so, shall be called least in the
kingdom of heaven; but he who does them and teaches
them shall be called great in the kingdom of heaven.

20 For I tell you, unless your righteousness exceeds that of the scribes and Pharisees you will never enter the kingdom of heaven.'

Explanation

In this section Matthew has fused sayings of Jesus which he found in existence into his own conception, and in this process has formed new logia. In the translation, the parts of the text which come from him are printed in italics. First I shall go through these verses in the order in which they appear in Matthew, and then at the end explain why Jesus did not speak any of these sayings.

[17] This verse derives from Matthew in its entirety. The beginning corresponds to the introduction in 10.34, which is similarly redactional. 'Fulfil' is one of the First Evangelist's favourite words. The phrase 'Law and Prophets' is also attested as Matthaean in 7.12 and 22.40. In principle 'fulfil' has a positive significance, as also emerges from the contrast with 'abolish'. It is possible that in v.17 Matthew is correcting a saying of Jesus which he regards as false: 'I have come to abolish the Law and the Prophets.' Compare Matt. 13.41, where the Matthaean interpretation of the parable of the weeds among the wheat mentions people who do lawlessness. Such a 'false' saying of Jesus could come from them.

[18] The introduction and conclusion give the verse a Matthaean character, whereas in the middle Q is probably the basis. Verse 18d, like Matt. 24.34, points to the end of the world.

[19] Matthew found this verse as an isolated saying and inserted it here. Perhaps the designation 'least' is an allu-

sion to the apostle Paul, who applies this description to himself (I Cor. 15.9). But it is still worth noting that he too enters the kingdom of heaven – albeit in a subordinate position. This could be an offer of union to the Gentile Christians under Paul's leadership. Perhaps Paul would even have been happy with it.

'The least of these commandments' probably refers to the teaching of Jesus presented from Matt. 5.21 on.

[20] Here Matthew concludes the sayings which have gone before with the word 'for' and an explanatory clause. At the same time he prepares for the following section. The attitude of righteousness required by 'Jesus' is the antitype of the caricature presented by the scribes and Pharisees.

Historical yield

The section is stamped throughout by Matthew's purpose and the problems in his communities. Jesus made none of these statements. (See also the previous section on Luke 16.17.)

Matthew 6.1–6, 16–18
Jesus lays down rules for piety

'1 *Beware of practising your piety before men in order to be seen by them; for then you will have no reward from your Father who is in heaven.*

First rule

2 Now when you give alms, sound no trumpet before you, as the hypocrites do in the synagogues and in the streets, that they may be praised by men. Truly, I say to

you, they already have their reward. 3 But when you
give alms, do not let your left hand know what your
right hand is doing, 4 that your alms may remain secret.
And your Father who sees in secret will reward you.

Second rule

5 And when you pray, you must not be like the hypocrites; for they love to stand and pray in the synagogues
and at the street corners, that they may be seen by men.
Truly, I say to you, they already have their reward.
6 But when you pray, go into your room and shut the
door and pray to your Father who is in secret; and your
Father who sees in secret will reward you.

Third rule

16 When you fast, do not look dismal, like the hypocrites, for they disfigure their faces to show people their
fasting. Truly, I say to you, they already have their
reward. 17 But when you fast, anoint your head and
wash your face, 18 that your fasting may not be seen by
men but by your Father who is in secret; and your
Father who sees in secret will reward you.'

Explanation

Three rules about piety form the core of this section. Their construction is symmetrical and each time they are introduced by a 'When' clause (vv.2, 5, 16). They deal with almsgiving (vv.2–24), prayer (vv.5–6) and fasting (vv.16–18). (Verses 7–15 have been inserted by Matthew and are not discussed here.)

The rules of piety have a structure deriving from

wisdom. They concentrate on a private piety. Public worship in the temple is not mentioned; the individual stands at the centre. Radical asceticism is called for as a personal religious attitude.

Matthew has put the introductory verse at the top as a heading for the whole section. Observations on the language suggest its redactional origin: thus the designation of God as the 'Father in heaven' and the term 'righteousness' are typically Matthaean. That means that the First Evangelist has deliberately put the following three rules of piety, which he possessed as a traditional catechism, under the theme of righteousness.

Historical yield

In no way did Jesus speak these words. *First,* they have nothing to do with his call to repentance, which is grounded in the imminence of the kingdom of God and his radical ethical demands. *Secondly*, the rules about fasting stand in direct opposition to the authentic saying of Jesus in Mark 2.19, according to which the presence of the bridegroom Jesus makes the observance of the commandments about fasting superfluous. By contrast, Mark 2.20 comes from the time after the death and 'resurrection' of Jesus. This states: 'The days will come when the bridegroom is taken away from them, and then they will fast in that day.' This is the situation in which rules about fasting like those in Matt. 6.16–18 could have been developed. But if these are inauthentic, because the form corresponds, the same is also to be said of the first and second rules.

3. Jesus forecasts his suffering and death

Mark 8.31; 9.31; 10.32b–34
The Markan predictions of the passion and resurrection

Mark 8.31

And he began to teach them: 'The Son of man must suffer many things, and be rejected by the elders and the chief priests and the scribes, and be killed, and after three days rise.'

Mark 9.31

He was teaching his disciples and saying to them: 'The Son of man will be delivered into the hands of men, and they will kill him, and when he is killed, after three days he will rise.'

Mark 10.32b–34

32 And taking the Twelve again, he began to tell them
what was to happen to him: '33 Look, we are going up
to Jerusalem; and the Son of man will be delivered to the
chief priests and the scribes. And they will *condemn* him
to death, and deliver him to the Gentiles 34 and they
will *mock* him, and *spit upon* him, and *scourge* him, and
kill him; and after three days he will rise.'

Explanation

The first prediction, which is the opening text (Mark 8.31), is the basis for the second and third predictions of the passion and resurrection. Mark has formulated the two other texts on the basis of this announcement of the passion and resurrection which had been handed down to him, giving the third prediction special weight by orientating the details contained in it closely on his account of the passion. Thus three verbs used in the passion narrative, 'condemn' (cf. 14.64), 'mock' (cf. 15.20,31), 'spit upon' (cf. 14.65; 15.19) appear in Mark 10.32b–34. (On 'scourge' cf. 15.15.)

By means of these three announcements of the passion (and especially the third), Mark wants to indicate that Jesus is going voluntarily to Jerusalem to die there; for this is necessary and accords with the will of his Father (cf. 8.31a). Jesus predicts his end right down to details yet nevertheless will not be diverted from his decision.

Perhaps there was also an edifying intent: only if Jesus knew of his death and resurrection in advance and predicted it is he really the Lord of death and life. We see the completion of this development in the Gospel of John (John 10.17–18): '17 For this reason the Father loves me, because I lay down my life, that I may take it again. 18 No one takes it from me, but I lay it down of my own accord. I have power to lay it down, and I have power to take it again. This charge I have received from my Father.'

As Mark links the third prediction of the passion so closely with the passion narrative, an anti-Jewish feature becomes clear in it (cf. also the sections Matt. 23.13–28; 21.33–46; 22.1–14 and John 8.37–45 which have already been discussed above). For with the killing of Jesus the Jewish authorities accomplish the plan they have been cherishing since the beginning of Jesus' public ministry.

Cf. Mark 3.6: 'The Pharisees went out, and immediately held counsel with the Herodians against him, how to destroy him.'

Historical yield

The clearly recognizable intent which Mark has in the *threefold* prediction of the passion and resurrection tells against its historicity.

Counter arguments against the assumption of the historicity of the *one* prediction of the passion and resurrection in Mark 8.31 are: *first,* its undisguised anti-Judaism. *Secondly,* it is hardly credible that Jesus spoke of his resurrection after three days, since this was an unhoped-for event for the first disciples. So the prediction of his own resurrection would have only been put into Jesus' mouth at a later stage. But in that case there is also considerable doubt about the prediction of his own suffering. In positive terms, Jesus went up to Jerusalem to see the coming of the kingdom of God or the new temple (cf. below, pp.104–8).

Mark 14.26–31
The announcement of Peter's denial

26 And when they had sung a hymn, they went out to
the Mount of Olives. 27 And Jesus said to them, 'You
will all fall away; for it is written, "I will strike the
shepherd, and the sheep will be scattered." 28 But after
I am raised up, I will go before you to Galilee.'
29 Peter said to him, 'Even though they all fall away, I
will not.'

30 And Jesus said to him, 'Truly, I say to you, today, this very night, before the cock crows twice, you will deny me three times.'
31 But he said once again, 'Even if I must die with you, I will not deny you.'
And they all said the same.

Explanation

This scene has been formulated in retrospect, using the tradition later developed widely in the Gospel of Mark that Jesus was denied by Peter before his arrest (Mark 14.66–72) and rose after his death (Mark 16.1–8). As the Son of God, Jesus must of course also have known these two future events in advance (cf. the three predictions of his passion and resurrection in the previous section). The same goes for Jesus' prediction that all the disciples would take offence at him (Mark 14.50). Significantly it is backed up by a quotation from scripture (Zech. 13.7).

Historical yield

The scene has been composed by Mark and is therefore certainly unhistorical. Jesus never spoke these words about Peter's future denial of him. The same is true of his statement that all the disciples would take offence at him.

Mark 14.17–21
The announcement of Judas' betrayal

17 And when it was evening he came with the Twelve.
18 And as they were reclining at table and eating, Jesus

said, 'Truly, I say to you, one of you who is eating with me will betray me.'
19 And they began to be sorrowful and asked him one after another, 'Is it I?'
20 He said to them, 'It is one of the Twelve who is dipping bread into the dish with me. 21 For the Son of
man goes as it is written of him; but woe to that man by whom the Son of man is betrayed! It would have been better for that man if he had not been born.'

Explanation and historical yield

The passage has the same relationship to Mark 14.43–45 (Judas betrays Jesus with a kiss) as does the previous section to Mark 14.66–72, which relates Peter's denial of Jesus. Jesus never spoke the words about Judas' betrayal.

4. Jesus gives the church authority to bind and loose

Matthew 18.15–18

'15 If your brother sins against you, go and take him to task, just the two of you. If he listens to you, you have
gained your brother. 16 But if he does not listen, take one or two others along with you, that everything may be confirmed by the words of two or three witnesses. 17
If he refuses to listen to them, tell it to the community. And if he refuses to listen even to the community, let him be to you as a Gentile and a tax collector.
18 Truly, truly, I say to you, whatever you bind on earth shall be bound in heaven, and whatever you loose on earth shall be loosed in heaven.'

Explanation

The section consists of two parts, vv.15–17 and v.18.

Verses 15–17 contain in the form of sayings of Jesus a disciplinary order for the community, giving rules for procedure in a conflict where a member has committed a sin. If no reconciliation is achieved, the brother is to be treated as a Gentile or a tax collector. It is illuminating that here the community is still living quite apart from the Gentiles (cf. similarly Matt. 6.7).

Outwardly the saying of Jesus in v.18 has been attached to vv.15–17 at a secondary stage, since it deals with another topic and has nothing to do with community discipline. At the same time it provides the necessary confirmation for the procedure in vv.15–17. According to Jesus' saying, God will confirm the community's verdict on the sinner who is not ready to repent.

Historical yield

Verses 15–17 are wholly rooted in a particular situation of the community after the death of Jesus and for that reason alone cannot go back to Jesus. The same is true of v.18, which – as a saying of Jesus – gives the community heavenly sanction for its effective jurisdiction.

Matthew 16.17–19

> 17 And Jesus answered him, 'Blessed are you, Simon
> Bar-Jonah! For flesh and blood have not revealed this to
> you, but my Father who is in heaven. 18 And I tell you,
> you are Peter, and on this rock I will build my church,

and the gates of hell shall not prevail against it. 19 I will
give you the keys of the kingdom of heaven, and whatever you bind on earth shall be bound in heaven, and
whatever you loose on earth shall be loosed in heaven.'

Explanation

This passage, which has been handed down only by Matthew, gives Jesus the decisive authority over discipline and teaching. This follows from the verbs 'bind' and 'loose' in v.19.

Historical yield

Jesus cannot have spoken these words, as he did not found a church. Rather, this is a saying of the 'Risen Christ' which has a basis in the fact that after Jesus' death Peter was actually the first to see the 'Risen Christ' (cf. I Cor. 15.5). The words printed above were then put into the mouth of Jesus by Peter himself or his followers and subsequently backdated by Matthew into the life of Jesus. They are inauthentic.

John 20.21–23

21 [The risen] Jesus said to them again, 'Peace be with
you. As the Father has sent me, so I send you.' 22 And
when he had said this, he breathed on them, and said to
them, 'Receive the Holy Spirit. 23 If you forgive the sins
of any, they are forgiven; if you retain the sins of any,
they are retained.'

Explanation and historical yield

Jesus never spoke these words on the disciplinary law of the early church. They are inauthentic. For the reasons see the comments on the two previous texts.

5. Jesus sends his disciples out on a mission

Matthew 28.16–20
An appearance of Jesus and a mission charge

16 Now the eleven disciples went to Galilee, to the
mountain to which Jesus had directed them. 17 And
when they saw him they prostrated themselves before
him; but some doubted.
18 And Jesus came and said to them, 'All authority in
heaven and on earth has been given to me. 19 Go therefore and make disciples of all peoples, baptizing them in
the name of the Father and of the Son and of the Holy
Spirit, 20 teaching them to observe all that I have commanded you; and look, I am with you always, to the end
of the world.'

Explanation

Verse 16 reports the execution of Jesus' command to the disciples, given through women, to go to Galilee to see him there (Matt. 28.10). In the meantime Jesus has been raised and therefore has been appointed Lord of heaven and earth by God (v.18). In this status he commands the disciples to make disciples of all peoples and to baptize them (v.19). This text, which concludes the Gospel of Matthew, has two focal points. *First*, the peoples are to observe the words of Jesus, the commands that he has given to the disciples in the Gospel, for example the commandments of the Sermon on the Mount (chapter 5–7), and thus to walk in the way of righteousness. *Secondly,* Jesus promises the disciples his presence to the end of the world, as he has already intimated: 'Where two or three are gathered in my name, there am I in the midst of them' (Matt. 18.10).

Historical yield

Quite apart from the fact that the 'Risen Christ' is speaking in this text, the words of Jesus are wholly rooted in the situation of a community after his death, which is now actively engaged in mission to the Gentiles and no longer addresses the gospel to fellow Jews. That was not always the case, as emerges from Matt. 10.5–6, where the disciples had still been sent exclusively to the lost sheep of the house of Israel and not to the Gentiles. The text presupposes a situation corresponding to that of Matt. 21–23, where the church of the Gentiles has taken the place of Israel. According to this theory unbelieving Israel is damned to hell because of the guilt which it has loaded itself with by killing Jesus and his messengers. Since the situation of the text is quite different from that of the life of Jesus, Jesus did not utter the words of the mission charge in Matt. 28.16–20 either. They are inauthentic.

6. Jesus forecasts that some of his disciples will survive until the coming of the kingdom of God

Mark 9.1

And he said to them, 'Truly, I say to you, there are some standing here who will not taste death before they see that the kingdom of God has come with power.'

Explanation

Mark 9.1 is an individual saying in the mouth of Jesus which Mark has joined to the previous section by a linking formula ('And he said to them'). Mark has attached the narrative of the transfiguration of Jesus (vv.2–11) to the saying (for the purpose of this see below).

The verse relates to the expectation of the end of the world, the positive counterpart to which is the dawn of the kingdom of God. This expectation is reinterpreted by the author of the Second Gospel: with the transfiguration of Jesus, which is related next, the kingdom of God has already come in power and has been seen by the three disciples Peter, James and John.

The saying which Mark has woven in here arose in the time after the death and 'resurrection' of Jesus when the expectation of the coming of Jesus from heaven was still alive, though some of his disciples had unexpectedly died. The saying of Jesus reassures these disciples who are still alive that at least a small remnant of the first generation will survive to see the dawn of the kingdom of God. They can rely on that.

The letters of the only eyewitness of the first primitive Christian generation, Paul, give us some insight into the problem of the 'delay of the parousia'. In I Corinthians 15.51 he relates a 'mystery' which he has experienced, i.e. a saying of the Lord granted to him as a prophet, which should solve the problems in the community. He writes:

> 'We shall not all sleep,
> but we shall all be changed.'

Then follows a description of the end which emphasizes its sudden appearance, puts stress on the trumpet of judgment, and confirms the raising of the dead (I Cor. 15.52).

This saying has to be read against the horizon of the primitive Christian expectation that the end of the world and thus the advent of the Lord Jesus from heaven were imminent. The saying alters this expectation to the effect that most will die, but some could count on surviving to the end (thus also Mark 9.1).

We find a preliminary stage of this changed expectation for the future in Paul's earliest letter, that to the Thessalonians (I Thess. 4.15–17). Here the saying of the 'Lord' granted to the prophet Paul runs as follows:

> '15 For this we declare to you by the word of the Lord, that we who are alive and are left until the coming of the Lord shall not precede those who have fallen asleep. 16 For when the command is given, when the archangel's voice and God's trumpet resound, the Lord himself will descend from heaven, and the dead who have died in Christ will rise first. 17 Then we who are alive

and are left will be transported together with them on the clouds into the air, to meet the Lord; and so we shall always be with the Lord.'

At the time of the composition of I Thessalonians Paul evidently presupposes that the majority of Christians, himself included, can reckon on surviving until the advent of Jesus from heaven, whereas a majority will die.

It follows from this reconstruction that *before* the composition of I Thessalonians Paul had assumed that *all* Christians would survive until the coming of Jesus from heaven; and in this expectation he may have put forward the Christian view which was usual in the first years after the death and 'resurrection' of Jesus.

Historical yield

The reconstruction of the origin of the saying in Mark 9.1 demonstrates its inauthenticity. At the same time, along with the evidence quoted from the letters of the apostle Paul, it makes clear the burning expectation of an imminent end in the first Christian generation. It can already be said here that this is best understood if Jesus himself counted on the coming of the kingdom of God in the immediate future.

Matthew 10.23

'When they persecute you in one town, flee to the next. Truly, I say to you, you will not have gone through all the towns of Israel before the Son of man comes.'

Explanation

The saying hangs relatively loose to its context in the Gospel of Matthew – one more reason for regarding it as a saying of Jesus which has been handed down in isolation. Matthew will have come across it and woven it into his Gospel in order to increase what Jesus says to the disciples about their future destiny (vv.17–25). Matthew has inserted vv.17b–22 here from Mark 13.9–12; vv.24–25 come from Q (= Luke 6.40 with parallels in John 13.16; 15.20).

This logion reflects a burning expectation of an imminent end. For the person who spoke it and those whom he addressed, it was bound up with the conviction that they would experience the day of the Son of man in their own lifetimes. This saying gives a date for the end of the world. With its statement that the disciples will not have to endure persecution for long, it contains the clear presupposition that none of them (or only a minority) will die. Otherwise it would have been meaningless to speak to the disciples like this. To that degree this text belongs to an even earlier time than Mark 9.1, which we have just investigated.

Historical yield

Some scholars, following Albert Schweitzer, regard this saying as authentic, since v.23b contains an unfulfilled prediction. This argument is not convincing, since a primitive Christian prophet could also have made a prophecy that was not fulfilled. However, the saying can be derived completely from the situation of the community after the death and 'resurrection' of Jesus. Missionaries would have been campaigning in Israel for belief in Christ and would have been exposed to many difficulties. Paul again provides a parallel: he instructs his communities beforehand about the persecution they are to expect because Jesus' advent is imminent (I Thess.3.3–4). A further consideration which tells against the authenticity of the saying is that a situation of extreme persecution or a flight of the disciples would hardly have been conceivable in the lifetime of Jesus.

Mark 13.30

> 'Truly, I say to you, this generation will not pass away before all these things take place.'

Explanation

The saying is closely related to the saying in Mark 9.1 (see above, pp.52–4) and could have been adapted on that basis by Mark himself for Jesus' discourse on the last things (Mark 13.5–37). Or it could have been inserted here as a saying about the date of the onset of the end. According to the saying, this date is the dying out of the first generation; here the first deaths in the community may have led to a modification of the imminent expectation. Although several Christians have not experienced the end, nevertheless the first generation will witness the coming of the Son of man. The most plausible explanation of the phenomenon here, that at least some of the first generation will not have to die, is that originally the the whole of the first generation were expected to experience the end of the age.

Historical yield

The saying reflects a delay in the end events. Accordingly Jesus expected the final advent of the kingdom of God in the immediate future. Therefore the saying in Mark 13.30 is certainly inauthentic.

John 21.22–23

> 22 (Jesus says to Peter about the Beloved Disciple:) 'If it is my will that he remain until I come, what is that to you?
> 23a The saying spread abroad among the disciples, 'This disciple will not die.'
> 23b Yet Jesus had not said to him, 'He will not die', but, 'If it is my will that he remain until I come, what is that to you?'

Explanation

Verse 23a reports the expectation that the Beloved Disciple will live until the parousia of Jesus. Nevertheless he died before Jesus had come again. The following solution was devised in his community: Jesus had not said that the Beloved Disciple would not die, but had merely asked what concern it was of Peter's if that was his will (vv.22 and 23b). That means that the error is corrected by a reinterpretation of the saying of Jesus concerned.

Historical yield

Verse 22 is not an authentic saying of Jesus. But v.23a, the earlier version of v.22, now corrected, is also inauthentic, since the word that is interpreted is one of those sayings about the end spoken by a primitive Christian prophet – not Jesus.

7. The sayings of Jesus on the cross

Mark 15.34

> 'My God, my God (Aramaic *Elohi, Elohi*), why have you forsaken me?'

Explanation and historical yield

Jesus' complaint corresponds word for word with Ps. 22.2 – with the exception that there God is addressed in Hebrew as *Eli*, whereas Mark has the Aramaic *Elohi*. Although Jesus spoke Aramaic, the very fact that Mark gives the cry of Jesus in its Aramaic version is an argument against its historicity. It is impossible for the Roman soldiers to have heard the words *Elohi*, etc., handed down in Aramaic, as a prayer to Elijah, as is reported in Mark 15.35: 'And some of the bystanders hearing it said, "Look, he is calling Elijah."'

But there cannot be witnesses other than the soldiers, since the women are said to have observed Jesus' death on the cross only from a distance (Mark 15.40f.) – that is, if this note has any historical value at all. Finally, two other reasons tell against the historicity of this cry of Jesus from the cross. *First*, contradictory prayers of Jesus on the cross have been handed down (see below). *Secondly*, it derived from the primitive Christian need to adorn the crucifixion scene with borrowings from the Old Testament. Here Psalms 22; 31 and 69 provided most of the material.

It was edifying to read the passion story in the light of the Psalter. It helped to overcome the offence that God's Son, who was daily present in worship, had had to drink the bitter cup of death.

Matthew 27.46

'My God (Hebrew *Eli*), my God (Hebrew *Eli*), why have you forsaken me?'

Explanation and historical yield

Matthew presupposes Mark 15.34 and changes 'Elohi' into 'Eli'. In so doing he is taking account of the biblical basis in Ps. 22.2 and explaining why the Roman soldiers could have heard Jesus' cry as a prayer to Elijah. The historicity of this cry can be ruled out because Matthew was using Mark's account as a basis and was not an eye-witness.

Luke 23.46

'Father, into your hands I commend my spirit!'

Explanation and historical yield

This sentence corresponds to Ps. 31.6 and derives from the early Christian tendency to interpret the passion of Jesus in the light of the Old Testament psalms. It is inauthentic.

Luke 23.43

'Truly, I say to you, today you will be with me in paradise.'

Explanation and historical yield

The verse gives Jesus' reply to the request of one of the two men who were crucified with him (v.42: 'Jesus, remember me when you come into your kingdom') and really presupposes the notion of an ascent of Jesus from the cross. Evidently the saying represents an attempt to overcome the problem of the delay of the parousia (see above, pp.52–4): Jesus' disciples do not get to heaven only at the end of the ages, which was the hope of the earliest Christian expectation, but immediately after death. (Luke did not note the contradiction between the ascent of Jesus from the cross and his ascent on Easter Day, Luke 24.51.) Now if the saying is indissolubly bound up with the problem of the delay of the parousia, it cannot possibly be historical.

John 19.30

'It is finished!'

Explanation and historical yield

According to John's theological conception, the passion of Jesus is the completion of the mission of the Son of God. Through his death on the cross he returns to the glory which he had from the very beginning as the Pre-existent One (cf.1.1ff.). John can even say that the crucifixion of Jesus is identical with his exaltation (cf. 3.14; 8.28) or his glorification (12.23,28; 13.31f.; 17.1,5, etc.). It is in keeping with this that even on the cross Jesus remains the Lord who is in command, unbroken and unshaken. For this reason the evangelist suppresses any cry of godforsakenness and instead makes Jesus utter the triumphant saying 'It is finished!' So the saying derives exclusively from John's overall christological conception and is therefore clearly inauthentic.

John 19.25–27
The mother of Jesus and the Beloved Disciple under the cross

25 Now standing by the cross of Jesus were his mother,
and his mother's sister, Mary the wife of Clopas, and
Mary Magdalene. 26 When Jesus saw his mother, and
the disciple whom he loved standing near, he said to the
mother, 'Woman, behold, your son!'
27 Then he said to the disciple, 'Behold, your mother!'
And from that hour the disciple took her to his own
home.

Explanation

In view of the precise enumeration of the women in v.25, which surprisingly also include the mother of Jesus, who is not mentioned at this point by the other three New Testament Gospels, it is striking that according to vv.26–27 the Beloved Disciple, who had not previously been mentioned, was also standing with them by the cross. That indicates that here John has dramatized an element from the tradition which dealt with the bond between

Mary and the Beloved Disciple, but which originally had nothing to do with the death of Jesus (vv.26–27), by connecting it with Jesus' last hours.

Historical yield

The scene cannot lay any claim to historicity. For first, in Mark 15.40f. (Matt. 27.55; Luke 23.49) the women observe what is happening on the cross *from afar*, and secondly, neither Jesus' mother nor a beloved disciple appears with the women near the cross.

Appendix to the sayings of Jesus on the cross
Mark 14.32–42
Jesus' prayer in Gethsemane

32 And they went to a garden which was called Gethsemane. And he said to his disciples, 'Sit here, until I have prayed.'
33 And he took with him Peter and James and John, and
began to be greatly distressed and troubled 34 and said
to them, 'My soul is troubled, even to death; remain here, and watch.'
35 And he went a little farther, threw himself on the
ground and prayed that, if it were possible, the hour
might pass from him, 36 and said, 'Abba, Father, all
things are possible to you; remove this cup from me; yet not what I will, but what you will.'
37 And he came and found them sleeping, and he said
to Peter, 'Simon, are you asleep? Could you not have
watched one hour? 38 Watch and pray that you may not

enter into temptation. The spirit is willing, but the flesh
is weak.'
39 And again he went away and prayed and said the
same words 40 and came back and again found them
sleeping; for their eyes were full of sleep, and they did
not know what to answer him.
41 And he came the third time and said to them, 'Are
you still sleeping and taking your rest? It is enough; the
hour has come. See, the Son of man is betrayed into the
hands of sinners. 42 Rise, let us be going; see, my
betrayer is at hand.'

Explanation and historical yield

To understand the text rightly, as in the discussion of the last cry on the cross we must free ourselves from the presupposition that this is the narrative of a conscientious historian. That is impossible, simply because no one was present at Jesus' struggle in prayer in Gethsemane. Rather, the *edifying* purpose of the whole episode must be evaluated rightly. The story emphasizes the obedience of the Son of God in contrast to the weakness of the disciples, since this Son of God is the Lord who is present in the worship of the community, and the community relies on him.

At the same time a parallel tradition to the Gethsemane scene shows the horizon of thought against which it is to be set. Hebrews 5.7 says of Jesus Christ, the Son of God: 'In the days of his flesh, Jesus offered up prayers and supplications, with loud cries and tears, to him who was able to save him from death, and he was heard for his godly fear.' This doctrinal statement derives from the reading of

Old Testament psalms like Pss.22; 31 and 69, which were also an important source for shaping the scene in Gethsemane and the passion narrative.

IV

Inauthentic Actions of Jesus

1. Jesus institutes the eucharist

I Corinthians 11.23–26

23 For I received from the Lord what I also delivered to
you, that the Lord Jesus on the night when he was
betrayed took bread, 24 and gave thanks, and broke it,
and said, 'This is my body which is for you. Do this in
remembrance of me.' 25 In the same way also the cup,
after the meal, saying, 'This cup is the new covenant
in my blood. Do this as often as you drink it, in
remembrance of me.' 26 For as often as you eat of this
bread and drink from the cup, you proclaim the Lord's
death until he comes.

Explanation

Preliminary comment: In a departure from previous procedure, the text printed above is not from the Gospels; it is a passage from the letters of Paul. These are around a generation earlier than the earliest Gospel (= Mark). The age of the text above becomes even greater when we note that Paul begins by stating that he himself has received the tradition which follows from the 'Lord'. In concrete terms, that means that the members of the community which he once persecuted and among whom he found a home in the new faith handed down to him the piece of tradition which is reported here. It was regarded as a saying of the 'Lord' because it was the basis of a constantly repeated custom and because the 'Lord' was himself present in the rite of eating and drinking.

The relationship between the eucharistic texts: the institution of the eucharist as a cult occurs not only in I Cor. 11 but also in Mark 14.22–25; Matt. 26.26–29 and Luke 22.15–20. Matthew has essentially taken over Mark's text and can therefore be left out of account in what follows.

The Lukan version of the words of institution is more extensive than that in Mark. In it the apocalyptic prospect of Mark 14.25 is prefaced with the saying over the cup (Luke 22.17–18). In close agreement with Paul's report quoted above, this is followed by the passage with the saying about the words over the bread and the cup (Luke 22.19–20). The Lukan version probably presupposes both Mark's account and the tradition in Paul. That means that to get to the earliest texts of the words instituting the eucharist we must define the relationship between the text preserved in Paul and Mark 14.22–25.

Mark 14.22–25

22 And as they were eating, he took bread, spoke the blessing, broke it, and gave it to them, and said, 'Take, *this is my body*.'

23 And he took a cup, and spoke the thanksgiving, and
gave it to them, and they all drank from it. 24 And he

> said to them, '*This is my blood* of the covenant, which is shed for many.
> 25 Truly, I say to you, I shall not drink again of the fruit of the vine until the day when I drink it new in the kingdom of God.'

Mark gives the words of institution in parallel – 'this is my body' (v.22); 'this is my blood' (v.24) – unlike Paul, who formulates them asymmetrically. At this point the words of institution in Paul are earlier, because they represent the more difficult version (in which body and covenant correspond).

Both the text of Mark and that of Paul contain an element which may have only accrued to the original tradition later. Mark 14.25 (see below, p.77) is an eschatological prospect of Jesus which has nothing to do with his gift of bread and wine. With I Cor. 11.26 the community looks towards the coming (again) of Jesus from heaven.

The text in Paul seems to be later than that in Mark at another point, namely in the twofold command to repeat the actions ('Do this in memory of me') in vv.24 and 25. For liturgical influences become evident in it, and these may only have accrued at a secondary stage. On the whole, however, the difference between the cultic formulae in Mark and Paul is not all that great, so that they can both be seen as the basis for the content of the account of the institution which we shall go on to ascertain.

Here it might be asked: how did the first hearers and readers understand I Cor. 11.23–25 and Mark 14.22–25? Doubtless they saw them as an account of the institution of the eucharist which they celebrated every Sunday and in which they received the body and blood of the Lord Jesus. This 'eating and drinking' was interpreted in many ways and in extreme cases was understood literally as the consumption of real flesh. See the interpretation of the eucharist in John 6.51b–58, especially vv.54–56, where Jesus says:

> '54 Whoever chews my flesh and drinks my blood has eternal life, and I will raise him up at the last day. 55 For my flesh is true food, and my blood is true drink. 56 Whoever chews my flesh and drinks my blood abides in me, and I in him.'

Others, like Paul, interpret the 'eating and drinking' as proclaiming the death of Jesus until his coming from heaven (see above on I Cor. 11.26). At all events it is certain that the significance of the eucharist was bound up with the situation *after* the death and 'resurrection' of Jesus, in which both were regarded as saving events.

Historical yield

Now if it is certain that according to the accounts of Paul and Mark (and the same is probably also true of the accounts of Matthew and Luke) Jesus celebrated the first eucharist with his disciples, and in it he distributed his body and his blood to them and they ate his body and drank his blood symbolically, really or in whatever way, then the institution of the eucharist described in this way is certainly unhistorical. The disciples could not have eaten Jesus' body and drunk his blood, since at the point in time when the eucharist was instituted Jesus had not yet died, and he had said nothing about a saving effect of his death or even his resurrection. Quite apart from that, the consumption of blood was strictly forbidden to Jews.

By contrast, the eucharistic texts take on meaning when they are read in the light of the liturgical practice of the earliest community.

2. Jesus performs nature miracles

Preliminary comment: all those actions of Jesus which intervene directly in nature and break the laws of nature are to be understood as nature miracles.

Mark 4.35–41
Jesus stills the storm

35 *On that day, when evening had come, he said to*
them, 'Let us go across to the other shore.' 36 *And they*
left the mass of people and took him with them in the
boat, just as he was. And other boats were with him.
37 And a great storm arose. And the waves beat into the
boat, so that the boat was already filling. 38 And he was
in the stern, asleep on the cushion.
And they woke him and said to him, 'Teacher, do you
not care if we perish?'
39 And he awoke and rebuked the storm, and said to
the sea, 'Silence! Be still!'
And the storm ceased, and there was a great calm.
40 *And he said to them, 'Why are you so fearful? Have*
you still no faith?'
41 And great fear came upon them, and they said to one

another, 'Who then is this, that even wind and sea obey him?'

Explanation

With this narrative, Mark, whose interventions in the tradition which came down to him have been printed in italics in the translation, emphasizes that Jesus stills the forces of nature with his word. The author had already accentuated the presence and nearness of the kingdom of God in the words or teaching of Jesus (cf. 1.14f.; 4.1–34), and later had repeatedly stressed the authority of Jesus' teaching. In addition, in v.40 Mark wants to say that the presence of Jesus is grasped by faith, although the disciples do not rightly understand the presence of the kingdom of God in Jesus' words. Mark is telling his readers about this, their faith.

The story relates a nature miracle which displays the typical elements of a verbal threat (v.39) and a description of its impact on the witnesses (v.41). The drama is heightened by the fact that not only does the storm pose great danger but the only person who could help is asleep and doing nothing (cf. Jonah 1.4–6).

Historical yield

The modern picture of the world has no room for this so-called nature miracle, and one cannot change one's picture of the world at will, like a costume: the attempt to take refuge in the ancient picture of the world simply because this is presupposed in the Bible is mistaken in every respect. Jesus did not still a storm, even if the early

Christians dreamed that he had and made it into a historical event.

Mark 6.35–44
Jesus miraculously multiplies loaves and fishes

35 And when the hour was already late, his disciples
came to him and said, 'This is a lonely place, and the
hour is already late. 36 Send them away, to go into the
places and villages round about and buy themselves
something to eat.'
37 But he answered and said to them, 'You give them
something to eat.'
And they said to him, 'Shall we go and buy two hundred
denarii worth of bread, and give it to them to eat?'
38 And he said to them, 'How many loaves have you?
Go and see.'
And they found out and said, 'Five – and two fishes.'
39 Then he commanded them all to sit down in table
groups upon the green grass. 40 And they sat down, the
groups like rows of vegetables, by hundreds and by
fifties.
41 And he took the five loaves and the two fishes and
looked up to heaven and gave thanks and broke the
loaves and gave them to the disciples to set before the
people; and he divided the two fishes among them all.
42 And they all ate and were satisfied. 43 And they took
up the fragments, twelve baskets, also full of the fishes.
44 And those who ate were five thousand men.

Explanation

Mark has reproduced almost unchanged a story which came down to him. He tells it again later in a similar way (Mark 8.1–9) – an indication of how important the miracle of the multiplication of the loaves and fishes was to him.

The narrative has the tripartite structure typical of a miracle story.

First, it describes the need of those present and their lack of food (vv.35–38); *secondly*, it reports how Jesus meets the need by miraculously satisfying the many people with the little that is there (vv.39–42); *thirdly*, the large amount of remnants (v.43) in comparison to the excessive number of those who have been fed (v.44) confirms the magnitude of the miracle.

The narrator emphasizes that here an unprecedented miracle took place which was even recorded in detail. At the beginning the disciples stated that they had only five loaves and two fishes. But when all had been satisfied, much more was left than was there at the beginning: twelve baskets full of pieces of bread and fishes.

Historical yield

The miraculous multiplication of bread and fishes did not take place. The reference by the early Christians to these and similar mighty acts of their 'Lord' derived purely from wishful thinking and was partly inspired by Old Testament stories of Elijah and Elisha (cf. I Kings 17.11–16; II Kings 4.42–44). This is true even though today theologians are in all earnestness attempting to rescue the biblical miracles by pointing out that the picture of the world offered by modern physics is an open one – a remark which is intrinsically justified.

Matthew 21.18–19
Jesus curses a fig tree

> 18 In the morning, as he (Jesus) was returning to the city, he was hungry. 19 And he saw a fig tree by the wayside, went to it, and found nothing on it but leaves only. And he said to it, 'May no fruit ever come from you again!' And the fig tree withered at once.

Explanation

Matthew uses Mark 11.12–14, 20–21 in telling the story of the cursing of the fig tree. He heightens the miracle by comparison with the Markan original: hardly has Jesus cursed the guilty tree than it withers. By contrast, in Mark there is a whole day between the curse and its fulfilment. That Matthew wanted to heighten the miracle also emerges from the verses which he has attached to the story of the cursing of the fig tree. Here 'Jesus' answers the disciples' question why the fig tree immediately withered with great boldness:

> '21 . . . Truly, I say to you, if you have faith and do not doubt, you will not only do what has been done to the fig tree, but even if you say to this mountain, "Rise up and cast yourself into the sea," it will be done. 22 And whatever you ask in prayer, you will receive, if you have faith.'

Historical yield

Jesus never cursed a fig tree (in the literal sense). If Matthew, following Mark, saw the fig tree as a metaphor for Israel, here too the historical verdict must be negative. Jesus never cursed Israel; the condemnation in the Marcan original (Mark 11.14) and other corresponding statements in Matthew (cf. above, pp.25–34) go back to the view of Christian communities after the death and 'resurrection' of Jesus. Their members took refuge in these nasty condemnations in their fight against non-Christian Jews, and without further ado attributed them to Jesus.

V

Authentic Sayings of Jesus

1. Beatitudes

Luke 6.20b–21

'20b Blessed are you poor, for yours is the kingdom of God.
21 Blessed are you who hunger now, for you shall be satisfied.
Blessed are you who weep now, for you shall laugh.'

Explanation

Poverty, hunger and suffering are not positive qualities for the person who speaks these words. But God will soon change for the better the fortunes of the poor, the hungry and those who weep, in accordance with the hopes of a royal ideal as this is expressed in Psalm 72:

4 The king is to 'vindicate the wretched, help the poor and crush the oppressors . . .
12 He will deliver the poor who cry for help and the wretched who have no helper. 13 He will have pity on the lowly and the poor, and will help the poor.'

The coming kingdom, which it makes sense to announce only if the distress will be transformed in the imminent future, is combined with the expectation of a festal meal.

Historical yield

Jesus spoke these beatitudes. This verdict is based first on the *criterion of growth*: in the Gospel of Matthew the beatitudes form a much longer series and there consist of ten individual blessings (Matt. 5.3–12). Then the *criterion of difference* also comes in: *(a)* If the beatitudes in Matthew (5.11–12) and Luke (6.22) speak of reviling and persecution (vv.11–12), and also refer to persecution (Matthew) or exclusion (Luke), they are focussed on the situation of the post-Easter community. (*b*) In addition Matthew spiritualizes the beatitudes by interpreting the poor as poor *in spirit* and interpreting the hungry as those who hunger and thirst *for righteousness* (cf. Matt. 5.3, 6). It emerges from this that in the earliest community the concrete material promises of Jesus were interpreted in a transferred sense. The reason for this lies in their radical and offensive nature. Moreover Christians increasingly recognized that the coming of the kingdom of God, which was finally to bring in the promised changes, was more and more delayed.

2. An eschatological eucharistic saying

Mark 14.25

> 'Truly, I say to you, I shall not drink again of the fruit of the vine until that day when I drink it new in the kingdom of God.'

Explanation

This saying has been attached secondarily to the account of the institution of the Lord's Supper (see above, p.67). In it Jesus expresses the expectation that he will drink wine again only in the kingdom of God, the underlying image of which here too is that of a feast. Thus the saying is at the same time a kind of prophecy of his death, which does not say anything about Jesus' future relationship to his disciples.

Historical yield

The *criterion of difference* supports the authenticity of this saying. It hardly came into being in the early community, since in it Jesus does not exercise any special function for believers in the feast in heaven which is imminent. Only Jesus' expectation of the future kingdom of God stands at the centre, and not Jesus as redeemer, judge or intercessor.

3. The petition for the coming of the kingdom of God in the future

Matthew 6.10/Luke 11.2

'Your kingdom come.'

Explanation

The prayer for the coming of the kingdom is the second petition of the Our Father, which as a Jewish – not as a Christian – prayer finds the sympathy of every Jew. Though there may be a dispute as to whether the whole prayer comes from Jesus, the second petition is certainly rooted in Jesus' preaching, if it may be referred to an imminent intervention by God.

Historical yield

The second petition of the Our Father, focussed on the end of the world which is to dawn soon, is an authentic saying of Jesus. In harmony with the basic structure of Jesus' preaching it points to a future kingdom (*criterion of coherence*). The use of the term 'come' in connection with the kingdom is relatively new in Jesus (*criterion of rarity*). It replaces talk of the coming of God, which can be found, for example, in the Old Testament (cf. e.g. Isa.35.4: 'Say to those who are of a fearful heart, "Be strong, fear not! Behold your God is here! He comes with vengeance, God who recompenses is coming and will help you"'). By contrast, the primitive Christian expectation was focussed on the coming of the Lord (cf. I Cor. 11.26; 16.22), so that the second petition of the Our Father cannot be derived from the earliest communities (*criterion of difference*).

Matthew 19.28

> 'Truly I say to you, in the rebirth (= resurrection of the dead) *when the Son of man shall sit on his glorious throne*, you who have followed me will also sit on twelve thrones, judging the twelve tribes of Israel.'

Explanation

The saying is an individual logion which Matthew has inserted into his text, developed in connection with Mark 10.28–30 (= Matt. 19.27, 29), to promise a reward to all those who follow Jesus. It promises that in the near future the twelve disciples will judge the house of Israel; here the clause printed above in italics probably derives from Matthew, because it largely corresponds to Matt. 25.31.

There is a similar saying in Luke 22.28–30; however, that, together with Matt. 19.28, is probably not to be attributed to Q, but similarly comes from oral tradition. It runs: '28 You are those who have persevered with me in my trials. 29 And I will assign the kingdom to you, as my Father assigned it to me, 30 that you may eat and drink at my table in my kingdom, and sit on thrones and judge the twelve tribes of Israel.'

Historical yield

At first glance the logion looks like a product of the 'Risen Christ'. For it is high-flying in its vision of the future, when one thinks that at the time of Jesus only two of the twelve tribes of Israel still existed: Judah and Benjamin. The other ten had been systematically broken up 700 years previously by the Assyrians.

On the other hand, fantasy is no sufficient criterion for historical judgments. And there is much to suggest the authenticity of this saying. *First*, it is closely bound up with the conception of the group of the Twelve. If the foundation of that group really goes back to Jesus (see below, pp.102f.), the logion indicates what significance Jesus attached to it: the Twelve symbolize the twelve tribes of Israel and predict their restoration in the near future. *Secondly*, this saying helps us to understand the Jewish side of Jesus better (*criterion of coherence*). Thus Jesus can be better understood as a Jew of his day who, like so many others, believed in the restoration of the twelve tribes of Israel (cf. Ben Sira 36.13; Psalms of Solomon 17.28–31; War Scroll of Qumran 2.2; 7.8; 5.1). Thirdly, the authenticity of the saying is supported by *the criterion of difference* (the logion cannot be derived from the early communities).

4. The presence of the kingdom of God in the experience and power of Jesus

Luke 10.18

'I saw Satan fall like lightning from heaven.'

Explanation

The saying appears only in the Gospel of Luke and describes Jesus' reaction to the return of the seventy disciples whose sending out by him has been described in Luke 10.1–12. Jesus' remark follows their report that even the demons are subject to them in the name of Jesus: 'I saw Satan fall like lightning from heaven.'

The saying gives the impression of being a fragment, since the miracles of the disciples and Jesus' vision hardly fit together; Jesus' vision and *his* miraculous power which follows from it would fit better. At the same time the saying is unique, in that only in it does Jesus appear as a visionary.

The overcoming of Satan in the *future* was expected in Judaism at the time of Jesus. Cf. the Ascension of Moses 10.1: 'And then God's rule will appear over his whole creation, and then Satan will be no more, and sorrow will be removed with him.' According to the speaker in Luke 10.18, what was expected in the Jewish tradition had already taken place in heaven.

Historical yield

The saying is authentic, since it cannot be derived from primitive Christianity (*criterion of difference*). There the victory over Satan was attributed to Jesus himself (cf. John 12.31; Rev.12.7). At the same time the *criterion of coherence* comes into play since, generally speaking, Jesus had intimate contact with the devil and with the demons subject to him. There is a legendary echo of this side of Jesus, which is often overlooked, in the temptation stories (Mark 1.12–13; Matt. 4.1–11 = Luke 4.1–13) and in the numerous reports of encounters of Jesus with demons who sense that he is near (cf. only Mark 5.1–20; Luke 13.32). The *criterion of rarity* can also be applied, since the future expectation on which the saying is based was very rare in the Judaism of the time as an event which has already taken place (by contrast see the quotation from the Ascension of Moses given in the section headed 'Explanation'). The end of the rule of the devil is the underlying conviction in Jesus' religious life.

Luke 11.20/Matthew 12.28

> 'But if it is by the finger (Matthew: spirit) of God that I cast out demons, then the kingdom of God has come upon you.'

Explanation

The logion comes from Q; 'finger of God' – instead of 'spirit of God' – certainly reproduces the original (Q) reading. For on the one hand the Matthaean version may be governed by the context, in which there is also a mention of the spirit of God (cf. Matt. 12.18 = Isa.42.1; Matt. 12.32), and on the other hand, given the significance of the spirit in Luke-Acts, it would have been inconceivable for Luke to delete this term. 'Finger of God' will be an allusion to the miracles of Moses before the exodus from Egypt (Ex.8.15). Here the Egyptian magicians recognize the superiority of Moses with the words 'That is the finger of God.'

Historical yield

The criteria of authenticity which apply to the logion Luke 10.18 (see above) are also to be applied to the present saying. The most famous New Testament scholar of this century, Rudolf Bultmann (1884–1976), thought that this saying could claim the highest degree of authenticity that can be made for a saying of Jesus. He said that it was backed by the eschatological feeling of power which must have governed the appearance of Jesus.

In his activity Jesus presupposes the fall of Satan. His exorcisms make that evident for him. The flight of the demons is a sign that the power of the evil one has been overcome, even if a final destruction of the evil powers will only take place in the final judgment, which is imminent. At the same time, the kingdom of God has already come, since the exorcisms are already constantly happening in the present, as the kingdom of God is gaining ground, irreversibly and visible to all.

Mark 3.27

> 'But no one can enter a strong man's house and plunder his goods, unless he first binds the strong man; then indeed he may plunder his house.'

Explanation and historical yield

The saying indicates that the strong man must first be overcome before his house can be plundered. If we may relate this statement to Jesus' battle with Satan, this means that that only if the devil has been defeated can Jesus successfully drive out the demons. To this degree victory over Satan and the expulsion of the demons govern each other. Both took place in the activity of Jesus *(criterion of coherence)*, so that the logion Mark 3.27 is to be regarded as authentic.

Mark 8.33

> He [Jesus] rebuked Peter and said, 'Get behind me, Satan! For you are not on the side of God, but of men.'

Explanation

The 'Satan saying' appears in a section (Mark 8.27–33) which contains the first announcement of the passion and resurrection of Jesus (v.31) and previously had related Peter's confession of Jesus as the Christ (v.29). But when Peter rebukes Jesus for his prophecy of the passion (v.32), Jesus addresses his first disciple as Satan.

Historical yield

In support of the authenticity of this saying of Jesus about Satan is its high degree of offensiveness (*criterion of offensiveness*). After the death of Jesus Peter was the leader of the primitive community, and during Jesus' lifetime he was his first disciple. Its offensive character also becomes evident from the fact that this verse is omitted from the Lukan parallel (cf. Luke 9.22). Matthew hands down the saying (Matt. 16.23), but relativizes it by the passage about building the church on Peter, which appears only in his Gospel (Matt. 16.17–19, see above, pp.48f.). However, the immediate occasion for this saying about Satan remains obscure and contrary to Mark's account might not be Jesus' prediction of his passion, since this has been inserted by Mark as redactor. At any rate the saying about Satan reinforces the impression that from the beginning of his public appearance Jesus had had intimate contact with the devil (*criterion of coherence*). This in fact clearly emerges from the authentic sayings Luke 10.18 and Luke 11.20/Matt. 12.28, which were investigated above.

5. The presence and future of the kingdom of God in the parables of Jesus

Mark 4.26–29
The parable of the seed growing by itself

26 And he said: 'The kingdom of God is as if a man
should scatter seed upon the ground 27 and should sleep
and rise night and day and the seed should sprout and
grow, he knows not how. 28 Of itself the earth produces
first the blade, then the ear, then the full grain in the ear.
29 But when it is ripe, at once he puts in the sickle,
because the harvest has come.'

Explanation

Mark has handed down the text of the parable unchanged. The focus of the parable is the contrast between the beginning and the end. Its point lies in v.28: the seed comes to maturity no matter what the circumstances – and does so almost automatically. The kingdom of God, a technical term in the preaching of Jesus, will establish itself soon, as is shown by the image of the harvest at the end (cf. Joel 4.13).

Historical yield

This parable goes back to Jesus, since he himself is not its subject (*criterion of difference*). On the other hand, the use of parables to speak of the kingdom of God is typical of the preaching of Jesus (*criterion of coherence*). The parable shows Jesus' rocklike confidence that in the immediate future God will finally bring in his kingdom, which is already present in the public appearance of Jesus.

Mark 4.30–32
The parable of the mustard seed
(cf. Matthew 13.31–34; Luke 13.18–19)

> 30 And he said, 'With what can we compare the king-
> dom of God, or what parable shall we use for it? 31 It
> is like a grain of mustard seed, which, when sown upon
> the ground, is the smallest of all the seeds on earth;
> 32 yet when it is sown it grows up and becomes the
> greatest of all shrubs, and puts forth large branches, so
> that the birds of the air can make nests in its shade.'

Explanation

The parable emphasizes the contrast between beginning and end. Jesus, who tells it, is convinced that God will bring in his kingdom from the most wretched beginnings, and will do so in the immediate future, since the image of the shrub which grows from the seed in v.32 is a technical term for a powerful kingdom which grants protection to its subjects (cf. Dan.4.9).

Historical yield

The passage contains the same message as the parable of the seed that grows by itself (see above) and is authentic (*criteria of difference and coherence*).

The parable of the leaven contains the same message, though without any explicit prospect of the end. It is printed here without explanation:

Luke 13.20–21 (Matthew 13.33)
The parable of the leaven

20 And again he said, 'To what shall I compare the kingdom of God? It is like leaven which a woman took and hid in three measures of flour, till it was all leavened.'

6. Jesus accentuates the Law

Mark 12.17

'Render to Caesar the things that are Caesar's,
and to God the things that are God's.'

Explanation

The saying is shaped by an accentuation of the first commandment (Exodus 20.2f.: 'I am the Lord your God . . . You shall have no other gods but me'). In answer to the question whether taxes are to be paid to the emperor, it does not call for a radical distinction between emperor and God in *all* spheres, a demand which the Zealots, the resistance fighters of the time, had inscribed on their banners. Rather, earthly things like taxes are owed to the earthly ruler, and to the heavenly ruler are owed heavenly things, i.e. probably obedience, service and love of him and one's neighbour. Whatever bears someone's image is his property and has to be given back to him: the money to the emperor and the whole person to God (Gen.1.27; 9.6).

Historical yield

The saying is authentic because it reflects the tendency in Jesus' preaching to accentuate the Law (*criterion of coherence*). At the same time the criterion of difference applies, because in this saying there is no teaching about Christ which has been shaped by the period after the 'resurrection'.

Matthew 5.22

> 'Every one who is angry with his brother shall be liable to judgment.'

Explanation

The saying is an accentuation of the fifth commandment (Exodus 20.13: 'You shall not kill'). However, it is not formulated as a prohibition, but as a statement of guilt.

Historical yield

The logion is authentic because it reflects the tendency to accentuate the Law in the ethic of Jesus and is rare in Judaism *(criteria of coherence and rarity)*.

Matthew 5.28

'Every one who looks at a woman lustfully has already committed adultery with her in his heart.'

Explanation

The saying accentuates the sixth commandment (Exodus 20.14: 'You shall not commit adultery'), but is formulated as a statement of guilt and not as a prohibition.

Historical yield

The logion is authentic and reflects the tendency of Jesus' ethic to accentuate the Law.

Matthew 5.34a

'Do not swear at all!'

Explanation

The logion derives from an accentuation of the Law which prohibited perjury (Lev. 19.12) and called for an oath to be fulfilled (cf. Ps. 50.14), without making the swearing itself a topic.

Historical yield

The saying is authentic. Various criteria apply to it:

(a) The *criterion of growth*, since the prohibition printed above is embedded in traditions which are familiar with an oath or a similar phenomenon: v.36 ('And do not swear by your head, for you cannot make one hair white or black') and the formula of asseveration in v.37 ('Let what you say be simply "Yes" or "No"') presuppose an oath or come very close to one.

(b) For the same reason the *criterion of difference* applies, all the more so since the absolute prohibition against oaths was not observed at all in primitive Christianity. Paul already swears often. Cf. Rom. 9.1: 'I am speaking the truth in Christ, I am not lying'; Gal. 1.20: 'In what I am writing to you, before God, I do not lie!'

(c) The absolute prohibition against swearing almost never occurred in the Jewish tradition. To this degree the criterion of rarity applies.

Matthew 5.44a/Luke 6.27

'Love your enemies.'

Explanation

The logion accentuates the command to love one's neighbour (Lev. 19.18) and is focussed on the extreme case, where the neighbour is the enemy.

Historical yield

The saying is certainly authentic, since there were divergences from it in primitive Christianity (*criterion of difference*): cf. the way in which the apostle Paul hates his enemies (II Cor. 11.13–15) and the hatred of the author of II Peter (II Peter 2.12–22). In addition, note that the author who transmits Jesus' command to love one's enemies has Jesus utter the hateful condemnations of Matthew 23 and even accentuates them (see above, pp.25–9). At the same time the saying that one should love one's enemy is rare within Judaism (*criterion of rarity*). The *criterion of coherence* also comes to bear here, since the saying again shows Jesus' radical ethic.

Mark 10.11–12
(cf. I Cor. 7.10–11)

> '11 Whoever divorces his wife and marries another, commits adultery against her; 12 and if she divorces her husband and marries another, she commits adultery.'

Explanation

The logion – often mistakenly claimed as a prohibition of divorce – prohibits remarriage after divorce. So the marriage continues to exist even after the divorce. Matthew 5.32 ('Everyone who divorces his wife, except on the ground of unchastity, makes her an adulteress; and whoever marries a divorced woman commits adultery') and 19.9 ('Whoever divorces his wife, except for unchastity, and marries another, commits adultery') presuppose this tradition, but allow remarriage after divorce in cases of unchastity. That is doubtless a further development on the basis of cases of unchastity which have happened.

It is uncertain whether v.12, which presupposes that the wife is the one who initiates the divorce, is part of the original saying. That question may be left open here. If the answer is negative, this clause would go back to Christians in the Graeco-Roman empire, for whom a separation initiated by the wife was more common than for Christians from the Jewish tradition.

Historical yield

The *criterion of growth* which is visible here, along with the criterion of rarity (divorce was a normal matter in Judaism) and the *criterion of coherence* (the radical nature of Jesus' ethic), show that the saying in its single or double form is authentic.

7. Jesus orientates the Law on human beings

Mark 2.27

> 'The sabbath was made for man, not man for the sabbath.'

Explanation

The saying is attached to a dispute between Jesus and the Pharisees (Mark 2.23–26). This gives an Old Testament example as the basis for the disciples' practice of rubbing ears of grain on the sabbath: David and his companions also ate bread from the temple, contrary to the Law, when they were hungry. By contrast, the saying of Jesus quoted above, which follows, justifies the disciples' practice by a general maxim. It is then followed by a further, christological, justification (v.28: 'Therefore the Son of man is Lord over the sabbath'). So the present logion appears in a series of three statements which justify the disciples' practice of rubbing ears of grain on the sabbath.

Historical yield

The verse is a key statement by Jesus. For he interprets the sabbath commandment and thus the Torah generally in the light of love, and the sacred tradition from the perspective of whether it serves human beings *(criterion of coherence)*. One day he expressed this in the provocative formula quoted in Mark 2.27. No wonder that both Matthew and Luke omit this statement (*criterion of difference*).

Mark 7.15

> 'There is nothing outside a man which by going into him can defile him; but the things which come out of a man are what defile him.'

Explanation

The logion is enigmatic, since in its context in the Gospel of Mark it is the basis for the disciples being allowed to eat bread without washing their hands (Mark 7.5). That is surprising, since the logion itself criticizes laws relating to food and not laws relating to cleanness. In modern terminology, rules about cleanness are connected with hygiene and relate, e.g., to menstruating women, lepers, and discharges from the male sexual organ (cf. Lev. 12–15). Food laws relate to nourishment and regulate the consumption of clean and unclean animals (Lev. 11). So the saying in Mark 7.15 has been handed down in isolation from the beginning and only later been inserted by Mark into this textual unit. Mark was led to do this by the consideration that eating unclean animals similarly made human beings unclean, so that in the broad sense the logion can also be regarded as criticism of the laws about cleanness.

Historical yield

The radical character of this saying is closely related to that of Mark 2.27, in that it undertakes a grandiose reduction (this time of the law relating to food). The authenticity of the saying is supported first by the *criterion of difference*, as the food laws applied without restriction in primitive Christianity, as is shown by numerous examples (Gal. 2.11–15; Acts 10; Acts 15.20, etc.). Moreover the *criterion of rarity* can be brought in to support the authenticity of the saying. As radicalism is also the hallmark of other statements of Jesus, in addition the saying meets the *criterion of coherence*.

8. Jesus issues a radical call to discipleship and comes into conflict with the Law

Matthew 8.22/Luke 9.60

'Let the dead bury their dead.'

Luke 14.26

'If anyone comes to me and does not hate his own father and mother and wife and children and brothers and sisters, yes and even his own life, he cannot be my disciple.'

Explanation

The sayings above come into conflict with the Law. For in Judaism there was an obligation to bury the dead. And to hate one's own family was quite contrary to the fourth commandment (Exodus 20.12: 'Honour your father and mother . . .').

Historical yield

Both sayings are authentic (*criterion of rarity*), and can also be explained by the disruption in Jesus' relations with his own physical family. According to Mark 3.21 Jesus' family thought that he was crazy and wanted to seize him. (Significantly, Luke and Matthew omit this offensive statement.) At the same time the *criterion of difference* applies, since the radical statements quoted above cannot be derived from the primitive Christian communities, with the possible exception of the Q group – if there was such a thing. These sayings must have ruled themselves out as soon as there were Christian families – and this happened very soon (see the examples in the letters of Paul).

9. Immoral heroes in the preaching of Jesus

Preliminary comment: This section, starting with a parable from the Gospel of Thomas, presents all the extant parables of Jesus which have immoral heroes. They are printed below without further commentary, and together with remarks about the life of Jesus lead into the chapter 'Authentic Actions of Jesus'.

Gospel of Thomas 98
The parable of the assassin

> Jesus said: 'The kingdom of the father is like a man who wanted to kill a powerful man. In his own house he drew his sword and stuck it into the wall in order to find out whether his hand was strong enough. Then he killed the powerful man.'

Explanation and historical yield

The verdict that this parable goes back to Jesus is based on the offensive nature of the parable: Jesus makes a murderer a hero. This offensiveness was probably the reason why the parable was not included in the New Testament, but fell victim to a moral censorship.

However, not all the immoral heroes in the parables of Jesus suffered the same fate: some appear at other points. Although they do not include murderers, we do find a criminal among them who deals irresponsibly with his master's possessions (the unjust steward, Luke 16.1–7); there is also a greedy treasure-seeker who does not share his treasure with others (Matt. 13.44); a successful master thief (Matt. 24.43–44; Luke 12.39); and a corrupt judge, who only changes his verdict in order to guarantee his own security.

However, Jesus did not just make immoral heroes the main characters in his parables. In a way his own life was that of an immoral hero. Occasionally he deliberately transgressed the sabbath commandment (cf. Mark 2.27 [above, pp.92f.]). He taught those who should have taught him. He called on the people to love those whom they really should have hated. In public he was regarded as a friend of tax-collectors and sinners, as a glutton and a drunkard (Luke 7.34). The life of Jesus was not that of a hero who went his way to victory without hindrance; his life was not the kind that had a happy ending. Jesus' condemnation, his death on the cross and the immediate failure of his activity formally made him the opposite of a hero. Putting all existing values in question and thus turning them upside down, he became an extremely immoral anti-hero.

And perhaps it was precisely the other immoral heroes, like toll collectors and prostitutes, who were among Jesus' hearers and who recognized themselves in his parables with all their strengths and weaknesses. Jesus challenged the pious of his time with his activity and his teaching and unmasked their pseudo-piety. For it was deliberately provocative to tell parables with immoral heroes. It put conventional rules in question and was an incentive to see things from another perspective. The immoral hero was a scandal and a model at the same time. It was appropriate that the immoral hero Jesus should make immoral figures his own heroes.

Is the parable from the Gospel of Thomas an invitation to open violence? Does it shows Jesus as a terrorist? Clearly in this parable Jesus is not giving advice about how a murder can be carried out successfully. Rather, the parable reflects a firm purpose: the resolution of the murderer to kill his opponent. Everyone should act in important things as unswervingly as this immoral hero.

Two attributes of the murderer stand out here. First, he

acts resolutely and purposefully; secondly, he acts wisely and makes sure that his action will be successful. Similarly, in another passage (Mark 3.27) Jesus is not anxious to give a tip about how a successful burglary can be carried out: 'No one can enter a strong man's house and plunder his goods, unless he first binds the strong man; then indeed he may plunder his house' (cf. p.83 above on the biographical background to this saying in the activity of Jesus).

Here the point of comparison is again the shrewd and purposeful behaviour of the thief: the plundering of the house presupposes that first of all the owner has been neutralized.

With the parable of the assassin from the Gospel of Thomas, Jesus may have wanted at the same time to make it clear to his hearers that the rule of God was certainly coming. The considered and resolute act of the murderer corresponds to God's resolve to establish his own kingdom. God will carry through what he has begun. The kingdom of God may not yet be here, but its fulfilment cannot be restricted or delayed.

However, for Jesus the kingdom of God at the same time represents a challenge to men and women. For in the face of the crisis which is imminent, Jesus calls on everyone to act thoughtfully and resolutely, to recognize the signs of the time and their own situation, and to know what is to be done. This is then to be carried out without delay and compromise. The coming of the kingdom of God makes this resolution and this sacrifice absolutely necessary.

Matthew 13.44
The parable of the treasure in someone else's field, or, The deceitful finder

'The kingdom of heaven is like a treasure hidden in a field, which a man found and covered up. And in his joy he goes and sells all that he has and buys that field.'

Luke 12.39
The parable of the successful thief, or, The master thief

'If the householder had known at what hour the thief was coming, he would not have let his house be broken into.' (Continuation, which has been broken off: 'But he did not know, and so the thief was successful.')

Luke 18.2–5
The parable of the godless judge

'2 In a city there was a judge who neither feared God nor regarded man. 3 And there was a widow in that city who kept coming to him and saying, "Vindicate me against my adversary." 4 For a while he refused. But then he said to himself, "Though I neither fear God nor regard man, 5 yet because this widow bothers me, I will vindicate her, or she will wear me out by her continual coming."'

Luke 16.1b–7
The parable of the shrewd steward

'1b There was a rich man who had a steward, and
charges were brought to him that this man was wasting
his goods. 2 And he called him and said to him, "What
is this that I hear about you? Turn in the account of
your stewardship, for you can no longer be steward."
3 And the steward said to himself, "What shall I do,
since my master is taking the stewardship away from
me? I cannot dig, and I am ashamed to beg.
4 I know what I shall do, so that people may receive me
into their houses when I am put out of the stewardship."
5 So, summoning his master's debtors one by one, he
said to the first, "How much do you owe my master?"
6 He said, "A hundred measures of oil." And he said to
him, "Take your bill, and sit down quickly and write
fifty."
7 Then he said to another, "And how much do you
owe?" He said, "A hundred measures of wheat." He
said to him, "Take your bill, and write eighty."'

VI

Authentic Actions of Jesus

1. Jesus submits to baptism by John the Baptist

Mark 1.9

In those days Jesus came from Nazareth in Galilee and was baptized by John in the Jordan.

Explanation

Jesus did not understand himself to be sinless. He had himself baptized by John 'for the forgiveness of sins' (Mark 1.4), and said that only God was good (Mark 10.17f.). The cross-check for the claim that Jesus saw himself as a sinner is provided by the First Evangelist, who reinterpreted the baptism of Jesus (Matt. 3.14: John to Jesus, 'I need to be baptized by you, and do you come to me?'); the Fourth Evangelist, who did not consider it to have taken place (cf. John 1.29–34: Jesus' baptism by John can be recognized only by those who know of it, but is deliberately omitted; 3.22f.; 4.1: John and Jesus baptize at the same time); and the Gospel of the Nazareans, which was not included in the canon. According to this last Gospel, Jesus expressly refused baptism from John: 'Wherein have I sinned that I should go and be baptized by him?' In other words, from a very early point in time, Jesus' estimation of himself as a sinner, which is visible behind the oldest tradition, is corrected in terms of the dogma of the sinlessness of Jesus.

Historical yield

The fact that Jesus' baptism by John is toned down or completely passed over in the later texts proves it to be historical (*criterion of difference*).

2. Jesus calls the Twelve and other disciples

Explanation and historical yield

There is no reliable text from the very earliest time which reports the call of the Twelve and other disciples by Jesus. But both are to be inferred as certain. Thus the call of the Twelve follows from Matt. 19.28/Luke 22.28–30 (see above, pp.79f.) and from the existence of the group of Twelve in the period *before* the conversion of Paul two years after the death of Jesus (cf. I Cor. 15.5: Christ appeared to Cephas, then to the Twelve). Any assumption that the group of Twelve had been called by the 'Risen Christ' and not by Jesus to some degree runs into chronological problems. It would then be necessary to explain why Paul himself had no kind of contact with the group of the Twelve, although this had only been constituted immediately before his conversion. In addition, nobody would have made Judas Iscariot a member of the Twelve after 'Easter'. It is therefore more probable that Jesus himself called the group of Twelve, which then remained in

Jerusalem during the first period of the primitive community but was eventually replaced by other entities like the three 'pillars' (James, Peter and John), with whom Paul had dealings in Jerusalem (Gal. 2.9).

The fact that disciples were called during Jesus' lifetime is certain, since otherwise it would be impossible to explain the explosive ongoing development of the group of disciples after 'Easter'.

3. Jesus drives out demons

Explanation and historical yield

No single story in the New Testament gives a correct account of the precise course of an exorcism by Jesus. But Jesus' authentic testimony to himself, investigated on p.82f. above, makes it certain that Jesus drove out demons. Cf. Luke 11.20: 'But if it is by the finger of God that I cast out demons, then the kingdom of God has come upon you.'

Further confirmation is provided by the observation that the latest Gospel in the New Testament, the Gospel of John, no longer relates a single exorcism of Jesus. Moreover it is worth noting that the newly-discovered Gospel of Thomas, which comes from around the same time as the Gospel of John (cf. above, p.13), does not contain any kind of reference to miracles of Jesus – far less exorcisms. And while Jesus' disciples are commissioned to do miracles (Gospel of Thomas 14), these do not include exorcisms, as still in the three earliest New Testament Gospels (Luke 9.2; 10.17ff.; Matt. 10.8; cf. Mark 6.13). These two facts also make it certain that Jesus performed exorcisms.

4. Jesus has contact with shady people

Explanation and historical yield

See the remarks on pp.95–8 above about Jesus' dealings with immoral heroes and the text:

Matthew 11.18–19a
(cf. Luke 7.33–34)

'18 For John came neither eating nor drinking, and they say, "He has a demon"'; 19a the Son of man came eating and drinking, and they say, "Behold a glutton and a drunkard, a friend of tax collectors and sinners."'

5. Jesus cleanses the temple

Mark 11.15–19

15 And they came to Jerusalem. And he entered the temple and began to drive out those who sold and those who bought in the temple, and he overturned the tables of the money-changers and the seats of those who sold pigeons. 16 And he would not allow any one to carry anything through the temple. 17 *And he taught, and said to them, 'Is it not written, "My house shall be called a house of prayer for all the nations"? But you have made it a den of robbers.'* 18 *And the chief priests and the scribes heard it and sought a way to destroy him; for they feared him, because all the multitude was*

astonished at his teaching. 19 *And when evening came they went out of the city.*

Explanation

The text is overlaid with Markan redaction, which is printed in italics in the translation above. The tradition used by Mark associates Jesus' appearance in the temple with his later execution.

Historical yield

It is not immediately clear what Jesus wanted to achieve with the action – that is, assuming its historicity in the first place. (a) Was it meant as a cleansing of the temple? But who could have regarded the driving out of the sellers and purchasers and the overturning of the tables of the money-changers and those who sold doves in this way? (b) Was it to be interpreted as temple reform? But that does not fit, since it did not affect the whole temple, but only a small area. (c) Jesus' action in the temple may have been more of a symbolic action pointing to something else. Jesus was attempting to do away with the temple cult symbolically. His action did not aim at reforming temple cult or stopping it from being profaned further, but at making room for a completely new temple, eschatological and thus expected by God *(criterion of coherence)*. There are two presuppositions for this understanding: 1. Jesus understood the overthrow (Mark 11.15) literally as applying to the whole temple; 2. he associated with it the hope of a new temple, various forms of which can be found in Judaism. Compare the following examples:

Isaiah 60.13:

'The glory of Lebanon shall come to you, cypresses, boxwood and pines, to beautify the place of my sanctuary; for I will make the place of my feet glorious.'

Micah 4.1–2a:

'1 In the latter days the mountain on which the house of the Lord is will be established higher than all the mountains, and be raised up above the hills. And the people will flow to it, 2 and many nations will come, and say, "Come, let us go up to the mountain of the Lord, to the house of the God of Jacob; that he may teach us his ways and that we may walk in his paths."'

Haggai 2.6–9:

'6 For thus says the Lord Sabaoth: "Once again, in a little while, I will shake heavens and earth, and sea and dry land. 7 Yes, I will shake all Gentiles. Then the treasures of all peoples shall come in, and I will fill this house with splendour," says the Lord Sabaoth. 8 "For the silver is mine, and the gold is mine," says the Lord Sabaoth. 9 "The new splendour of this house shall be greater than the former," says the Lord Sabaoth, "and in this place I will give peace," says the Lord Sabaoth.'

I Enoch 90.28f.:

'28 I stood up, to see until he wrapped up that ancient house. All the pillars were removed; all the beams and ornaments of that house were wrapped up with it. It was

> taken out and put in a place in the south of the land. 29
> I kept looking until the Lord of the sheep brought a new house, greater and loftier than the first one, and set it up in the place of the first one which had been wrapped up. All its pillars were new, the ornaments were new and larger than those of the first old one which he had removed. And the Lord of the sheep was in it.'

There is a further reflection of Jesus' criticism of the temple in the account of his trial. Cf. Mark 14.58: 'We heard him say, "I will destroy this temple that is made with hands, and in three days I will build another, not made with hands."' It is very probable that this logion about the temple derives from Jesus (cf. John 2.19; Gospel of Thomas 71), all the more so since Mark 14.57 expressly depicts it as false testimony (cf. Acts 6.15, to which it has been transferred by the author of Acts – probably to tone it down) and thus in this context robs Jesus' radical preaching of its point. Furthermore, it is also easy to understand Jesus' expectation of the heavenly temple in so far as the primitive Jerusalem community identified itself with the temple. Its members were constantly in the temple (Acts 2.46; 3.1ff.; 21.26), and here, in accord with Jesus, they expected the end of the ages.

I have not explicitly used elsewhere in this work the criterion for discovering authentic sayings and actions of Jesus used on this last point. It is a kind of *criterion of development* which in each case allows us to follow the development from Jesus to the early church. I nevertheless use it at the end of the book to indicate that the criteria alone are not sufficient in the question of the historical

Jesus. As Julius Wellhausen (1844–1918) once remarked, it ultimately depends on one's predetermined notions. To this degree I remain open to new insights into the origin of the early traditions about Jesus and their presuppositions.

Postscript

The final result of this journey through a selection of New Testament texts is sobering. It casts light on the brutal reality of the first century: the process of falsifying and overpainting the man Jesus, his words and actions, began in earliest Christianity and is already at an advanced stage in the New Testament.

Here it should be noted that in the present work approximately equal space has been given to the authentic and the inauthentic words and actions of Jesus. But it should certainly not be inferred from this that the authentic and the inauthentic words and sayings are also in balance in the New Testament. Rather, this book quotes around half of all the authentic sayings and actions of Jesus, whereas the inauthentic sayings and actions presented here represent only a small selection from a wealth of inventions.

In other words, both the number and the content of most traditions which have been preserved about Jesus, and which all claim to give authentic testimony about him, are in blatant contradiction to what he really said and did. The fact that the sayings were regularly spoken by prophets in Jesus' name as an inspiration from the 'Risen Christ' does not help, since Jesus did not rise, and therefore there is no such thing as the 'Risen Christ'. The historical judgment must be that the early Christians tailored Jesus to their wishes and interests, and in whatever way seemed to them to be most useful in the fight against deviants and those of other beliefs. Granted, the Christians of that time had practically no sense of historical truth, but that does not alter the fact that objectively they produced 'sacred lies'. For in antiquity people were well aware of the difference between authenticity and inauthenticity, truth and forgery. Philologists trained in Alexandria would certainly have seen *behind* the pious deception of the New Testament evangelists. And they would have been dismayed to see the way in which the early Christians turned the charismatic exorcist Jesus into someone who performed quite monstrous miracles; how they transformed the Jew who told parables into a resentful anti-Semite, who just did not want to be understood by 'those outside'; and how finally they elevated the restless itinerant preacher into the ruler of the world who one day will pass judgment on the dead and the living.

Thus over wide areas of the New Testament the overpainting has distorted Jesus to such a degree that it is impossible to recognize him. Only here and there do fragments of his message glimmer through, and only at a few points can we still have an inkling of a shadowy outline of his person.

Furthermore, the falsification of the person and message of Jesus does not just pour scorn on any sense of truth; it has also been bought at too dear a price. However, it was the Jews, not the Christians, who had to pay the bill. For *they* were the ones who had to bear the expenses of the grand feast in the course of which inauthentic sayings and actions of Jesus were invented, and authentic sayings and actions of Jesus were perverted without any inhibitions. The triumph of the Christian church was and is the tragedy of Israel.

In conclusion, it must be emphasized that the discovery of the great deception which has been committed in the name of Jesus does not necessarily lead to resignation or despair today. For any scholarly negation is at the same time a positive act of the mind which prepares the way for something new. To begin with, we cannot do other than protect Jesus against all that the first Christians have made of him. What is left is indeed too little to build a Christianity on, especially as we would then have to understand Jesus contrary to his own intentions, and furthermore gloss over his erroneous expectation of the future.

So all that is left is for us to look forward. Here only enlightenment can prepare an abiding place for the life which pulses all over this earth. It leaves heaven for these who long for it: the angels, the sparrows, and the Christians.

Index of texts discussed

References printed in *italics* are to authentic sayings and actions of Jesus; those printed normally to inauthentic sayings and actions.